success
mapping®

Achieve What You Want . . . Right Now!

Arlene Johnson

GREENLEAF
BOOK GROUP PRESS

Published by Greenleaf Book Group Press
Austin, TX
www.gbgpress.com

First published in 2009 by Emerald Book Company

Distributed by Greenleaf Book Group LLC

For ordering information or special discounts for bulk purchases, please contact Greenleaf Book Group LLC at PO Box 91869, Austin, TX 78709, 512.891.6100.

Design and composition by Greenleaf Book Group LLC
Cover design by Greenleaf Book Group LLC

Publisher's Cataloging-In-Publication Data (Prepared by The Donohue Group, Inc.)
Johnson, D. Arlene-
   Success mapping : achieve what you want—right now! / Arlene Johnson.—2nd ed.
   p ; cm.
   ISBN: 978-1-60832-139-1
1. Success—Psychological aspects. 2. Self-actualization (Psychology) 3. Success—Handbooks, manuals, etc. I. Title..
BF637.S8 J64 2009
158   20009927329

Printed in Canada on acid-free paper

10 11 12 13 14 15 10 9 8 7 6 5 4 3 2 1

Second Edition

*Dedicated to
those who want to experience more
of life's possibilities.*

contents

Introduction

RIGHT NOW, WITHOUT ANOTHER THOUGHT, decision or action, realize this: You are totally and perfectly wired in mind and body to experience success in all aspects of your life.

Whether or not your life has looked like one of abundance, you have all the personal power you need to create and live the life you want. In your professional and personal life you can enhance what works for you right now, change what doesn't and achieve more of what has always been possible but elusive for you now…this moment.

On a gut level, can't you just feel it? You know you're designed to succeed, to experience more of life's possibilities. It's like jumping off a scooter to go full throttle in a Porsche. You've got the power. You've got the fuel. All you need is the map to show you the best route to get you there

If you have a yearning, passion or vision unfulfilled in your heart and mind, now's the time—the right time—to put action to that feeling and move forward to whatever you want to protect, to change or to achieve.

Why does this often seem so difficult? Why not be quicker to use the power of your energy to be thankful for all that you have now as you move forward to achieve all you want?

In my many performance coaching conversations, I've never met anyone who didn't want to experience greater success in some aspect of life. It wasn't that these individuals didn't want to protect what they had or accomplish something different. The challenge was that they either didn't believe they could or they didn't know how. Well, *Success Mapping* will show you how!

For several years, my intention has been to help others realize more of what they are innately capable of: their full potential. Writing *Success Mapping* became an important goal to accomplish to help me achieve this intention. However, I procrastinated and made excuses (albeit subtle ones) for not completing this book. I was guilty of starting-stopping longer than I care to admit.

It took watching a friend deal with a personal health challenge to move me into action.

Diane had been diagnosed with a serious illness. Her husband was understandably upset and sent an e-mail describing the situation to her friends. After reading it, I fully expected her to be devastated with worry and fear—but not Diane.

Throughout her recovery, Diane used the same life approach and plan she had used to accomplish her business and personal goals.

As she explained, "It doesn't do me any good to focus on my fears or anything else that could block me from recovering! Here's my plan: All my thoughts, feelings and actions are focused on good health and total recovery."

We often delay accomplishing what we want because we think, "Well OK, I've got lots of time, I'll start that later." Diane's illness made her understand, acutely, that time is precious. One year later, I am happy to report that she is healthy and is keenly aware of the value of being thankful for what she has now as she moves forward with what she wants to accomplish. As Diane said, "If you have a dream or there's something you want to achieve—start now!"

And I did, I got serious and developed my own Success Map, making the decision and taking the actions I needed to take to complete *SuccessMapping*.

Your Success Map

So, let me ask you, are you waiting to begin the process of achieving an important life dream or goal? If so, there must be no more excuses, delays or stops. If you want to enhance what you value now, create change or achieve something much more important to you, now's the time to make it happen!

 IMPORTANT

Use your **Success Map**, found in **Appendix Three**, as a summary and guiding document to compile all important decisions and actions as you move through the eight progressive steps of *SuccessMapping*.

Your Eight Steps to Success—Let's Get Started!

Developing your Success Map is simple: Believe in yourself and get started. The eight progressive steps of *Success Mapping* will be your guide to help you more easily accomplish an important life objective, step by step!

Whether you are a student or CEO, as you move through each Step you will gain the information and tools to recognize and move past the eight Success Blockers that if you are unaware can predictably prevent your success. Each Step guides you and keeps you focused to start, stay engaged and complete what you intend to achieve.

To help you track and monitor how you're doing with your Success Map, there is a Checkpoint at the end of each Step.

When you can answer Yes to a Checkpoint, you will know you are ready to proceed to the next Step in your Success Map. If your answer is No, that's also good to know. A No will help you check your progress and change course direction if necessary to achieve what you want in your expected timeline.

Using the Success Map is like traveling across the country with the most direct route and the best places to stop already mapped out. You keep moving in the right direction, and you've built in time to stop and enjoy the trip.

Same trip without a map? One wrong turn and, Oops, detour! You are using up your time and resources and you're headed in a direction that does not help you achieve your goal. Perhaps it's an interesting life detour, but it's a detour nonetheless.

With each Step Checkpoint you're able to assess: "Am I on track to achieving my goal?" and "Which action in my Success Map, when accomplished, becomes a reason for me to stop and celebrate?"

Above all, remember that success, ongoing success, is a process that will help you protect what you value now and enable any change you need to take to experience more of what matters most to you. *Success Mapping* will focus your energies on the right actions at the right times to overcome any setbacks or potential obstacles in your path as you expand your professional and personal horizons.

So, if you're ready . . . let's build your Success Map to achieve your life dream or goal!

step
one

What Do You *Really* Want?

The purpose of Step One in *SuccessMapping* is to help you:

- Be more aware of the scope of your possibilities.

- Focus on exactly what you want to accomplish.

- Reframe what can *prevent* to what can *enable*.

- Assess: "How achievable is what I want to accomplish?"

With a belief in your potential, all things are possible.

DO YOU HAVE A BUSINESS OR PERSONAL GOAL or objective you've wanted to achieve, but haven't?

If you asked yourself this question and then found your mind racing with various reasons of *why not*—no time, no support, no money—that would be normal. These excuses may not be the *real* reason, but it's certainly normal to think they are.

The human mind is capable of extraordinary innovation and accomplishment. History has shown us that, and daily we see evidence of it as others achieve new levels of business and personal success . . . sometimes against all odds.

The nation witnessed the first African-American to achieve the highest office in our country. With his intention and messages consistently focused on leading change, his voice resonated with the majority and he won, against all odds.

If you or someone you know has been bitten with the entrepreneurial bug, has started a business, and still has the doors open after five years, statistics on business closures tell us that he or she has succeeded, against all odds.

When cellular technology was a new industry, I got bitten by the entrepreneurial bug and left a great job with a great boss who paid me a great deal of money. Once bitten, apparently all common sense flew out the window. So, I left my cushy job, sold all my earthly belongings, moved to a new market, and founded a cellular company. Rather quickly it became evident why statistics show that more than 25 percent of start-up businesses close the doors within twelve months.

Starting a business in a new industry with limited funds and zero experience should have been a flag for me. It certainly was for my banker and product manufacturers. Trusting business partners to deliver on agreements without airtight contracts—well, that was a bit idealistic. And it almost cost me my company. But truth be told, being the only female principal in the country in the new cellular industry not only was a boost to my weary ego but also gave the company a competitive edge with much-needed media attention. So all in all, even considering some nerve-racking events, my reward was many priceless business experiences. And against all odds, I sold the business for a profit in a highly volatile and competitive market.

So for the moment, set aside your reasons—no time, no support, no money—for why you're not pursuing a life dream or goal. Why? Because following the Steps of *SuccessMapping* will guide you in overcoming any potential stumbling block.

The Power of Belief

Let's look below the surface reasons to flush out any underlying reasons for your delay in going for your life dream or goal, by answering these two questions:

- Why might you hesitate, delay, or just plain stuff your dreams into a back corner of your mind?
- What is your self-belief about what you can or cannot achieve?

Check it out. Think of something you want to achieve, write it below, and then respond to the question "Do I believe I can accomplish that?"

_____

_____

1	2	3	4	5	6	7	8	9	10

Using a scale of 1 to 10, how would you rate your response? A rating of 5 and below indicates a range from "I'm not sure" to "No way can I do that!" A rating of 6 and above indicates a range from "I think I can" to "Of course I can!"

Success Blocker: *Neglecting your potential.* Not believing that you can succeed with—or, because of multiple options, having no clarity about—what you *really* want to accomplish.

Regardless of what you want to achieve, your age, gender, race, or life situation may not be the roadblock to your success. If you don't *believe* you can . . . that's your *real* success blocker.

Your potential is much greater than you realize.

You have the capability, with countless life opportunities, to harness and use more of your innate human potential. What is available to each of us is far beyond what we imagine, acknowledge, or access. So, if you choose not to believe that you do indeed have tremendous unclaimed potential, your personal success could remain elusive, and your dreams and goals unfulfilled.

Are your beliefs of what you can or cannot do cast in stone? If so, science has news for you.

The science community provides abundant data and proof of your human capability. The research findings of quantum physicists explores how the basic building blocks of the universe work, how you are connected to them, and the vast potential that you have to affect your own reality— including your belief system—and the reality of the world around you.

Neuroscientists, who study the systems and function of the brain, have proven that your brain has the ability to change, learn, relearn, and recover from brain disease and injuries. This ability of your brain to interact in dynamically changing ways with experience is called *neuroplasticity*.

Gone are the days when the medical and science community saw the brain as hardwired and static. It is no longer assumed that your brain cells decline at a certain age or that physical or learning challenges caused by genetics or injury are inevitably permanent. This significant paradigm shift has huge implications for human potential. There is now research-based proof that your mind is capable of higher cognitive powers!

The plasticity of your brain gives you extraordinary capabilities. Your change-adaptive brain is composed of billions of nerve cells that constantly form new neural systems to aid in new learning and recovery processes. Neuroplasticity work with patients has resulted in artificial limbs that move with thought, hearing and eyesight regained because of newly formed neural paths, recovery of stroke patients, learning disorders eliminated in children and adults, cognitive skills improved, the effects of old age impeded, memories sharpened, and much more.

What this means for you is this: no matter how convinced you are that your perceptions of your limitations are correct and irreversible, you can literally *change your mind.* The ability to change your mind is linked to keeping your brain fit and flexible. If you are of the Baby Boomer generation and feel a twinge of concern about protecting your independent lifestyle in the upcoming years, such as driving and remembering where you are going, then Dr. Michael M. Merzenich has the answer for you.

Dr. Merzenich, a neuroscientist and professor emeritus at the University of California, has numerous honors recognizing his substantial contributions in the study of brain plasticity. He now serves as chief science officer of Posit Science, a leading provider of clinically validated brain fitness programs. Yes, that's right. Brain fitness programs. It is understood today that your brain is as plastic as your muscular system or your waistline. You can literally change your brain by what you do.

Your mental capacity for learning, adapting, and growing is astonishingly large. The science community has proven that, yes, you *can* learn new tricks!

Although research proves that neuroplasticity is what enables us to keep on learning, it also shows that the brain's plasticity can be diminished by rigidly held beliefs or the lack of new experiences. The old saying could never be truer: "Use it or lose it."

There is now a wealth of information as well as proven methods for training your brain for increased learning and good health. If you are interested in exploring the fascinating subject of you and your brain, here are two suggestions: Read *The Brain That Changes Itself: Stories of Personal Science from the Frontiers of Brain Science,* by Norman Doidge, M.D., or go to www. PositScience.com.

With all that is available, there is no excuse for not living life abundantly! A question for you to explore is "How might I experience more of my potential, right now, in my work and personal life?"

Keep mentally healthy and sharp.

Don't neglect your most important body part, your brain:

- Be a passionate learner—everyday, learn something new; then share with or teach others.
- Be curious and innovative—expand how you think by having conversations with different people; seek different or new solutions when problem-solving.
- Be a strategic thinker—weed out needless and energy-zapping activity and focus on your most important decisions and actions.
- Take intentional action—everyday, to move forward and stay on track to achieve a life dream or goal.
- Consciously choose—thoughts, behaviors, friends, and colleagues that support your success.
- Take time to play—with music that cause you to dance, with people or games that cause you to laugh, and with puzzles or games that cause you to think differently.
- In overload, take a break—block out five uninterrupted minutes to be still, listen to your breathing and relax.
- Take care of the heart and mind—be kind and caring with self and others, deepen and nurture meaningful business and personal relationships.

Your life options and possibilities are limited only by your self-belief of your capabilities. So, with your intention to place no limits on what you can accomplish with your present career, new business venture, education, or personal life, *SuccessMapping* will guide you, step by step, toward what you next want to achieve.

Options, Options . . . Decide What You Want

Having a plethora of options does come with challenges. Ask any student entering college for the first time. With so many academic and career track options available, it's not always easy to know which course or career to pursue. A student entering freshman year without knowing exactly what he or she wants to accomplish with a college education can end up changing majors, paying for college for five years instead of a planned four, and/or losing interest and having the grades to prove it—or even worse, dropping out. In one way or another, all the potential consequences are quite costly.

Many universities have provided a wide array of academic and career guidance support to help their students make the right decisions earlier. In a conversation with the dean of the business department of a major university, I learned about the department's flagship program to better prepare its students for the business world, beginning day one of their freshmen year.

Here's what he said: "We had a collective challenge, with the multitude of academic and career options freshmen students have . . . They were entering college not knowing what they wanted to accomplish, and they left college not knowing how to apply what they learned. We had to do something different, so we took on that challenge by aligning our business school track with professional development tracks."

He discussed the impact of students not knowing what they wanted to accomplish: "It's a huge opportunity cost to the student. Rarely are they in the 35 percent who graduate in four years. It generally costs them another year of school, and that also means a year of lost income."

Then he added, "We have observed a key indicator—poor academic performance—when students do not have a specific goal. Unfortunately, this can lead to a recommendation for their temporary withdrawal from college.

"There's no doubt, if you don't know what you want . . . college can be an expensive place to find yourself," he stated. "However, with or without our guidance, if students determine what they want to achieve during and after college, we'll help them get there. Their intention helps us design a clear road map for them to stay on track and succeed, including a four-year degree plan aligned with eight semesters of career development classes and mapped-out summers and introductions into our corporate pipelines. Our flagship program prepares students to be successful in the major or industry of their choice."

Regardless of your specific situation, if you're not really clear on what you want to achieve next, you run the risk of wasting time and energy with a detour in our business or personal situations. To help you achieve what you want, decide and focus on exactly what you want to achieve next in your career or personally.

What do you really want to accomplish?

So, thinking about your life possibilities and the many ways you could spend your time and energy—what matters most to you at this time?

Answering these questions is the first step in you knowing two important things:

- What do you want to do more of, change, or accomplish?
- Are your thoughts, feelings, and actions focused on achieving that goal?

Once you've answered these questions, your Success Map becomes your personal guide to keep you on track and moving forward until you achieve your desired goal results.

SuccessMapping is constructed with a strong yet flexible foundation. It guides you, step by step, to your next achievement. Moreover, if you choose to change directions, the Steps of your Success Map provide the flexibility to make the change and still keep you on course, moving toward your desired outcome, with no delays or lost momentum.

Understand the importance of structure for your personalized Success Map.

The value of the structure of the Success Map cannot be overemphasized. It strengthens your ability to keep distractions, emotions, and surprises from derailing you. It enables you to focus on the next important thing to decide or take action on in order to achieve what you want. Thus, building a plan designed for success requires a strong yet flexible foundation—like what you find in a well-constructed building. I learned the importance of this firsthand during an earthquake.

When the earthquake hit, I was on the nineteenth floor of a hotel in a foreign country. The building swayed side to side with an eerie creaking sound as cracks knifed across the ceiling. Who knew the movement of a building could make such terrible sounds?

People talk about experiencing raw fear. I now know what that means. Although the tremor lasted less than three minutes, it felt much longer. The effect of that 7.2-magnitude earthquake was devastating. More than 200 lives were lost, and there was massive damage to buildings, homes, and parks.

What saved us? My hotel and surrounding newly constructed buildings survived the quake because of the *intention* of the architect's design. The buildings were constructed to withstand, with relatively minimal damage, any movement under the foundation. Fortunately, the foundation was designed to be strong and flexible.

With this scenario in mind, place yourself in the role of architect, designing your own life experience. Once you decide what you want to achieve, your intention for what you want to be and do in your business or personal life will provide the focus and stability you need to move forward.

Your Success Map has the structure of strength and flexibility, leaving you free to focus on the best decisions to make next and the actions to take to ensure success.

The *strength* becomes evident as you make progress in accomplishing your goal with each completed Checkpoint. And the *flexibility* becomes evident as you move through each Step and have opportunities to make any needed changes, redirections, or additions to your Success Map.

With each *SuccessMapping* Step, you're moving forward with momentum to help yourself achieve this and other life dreams or goals. And that's exciting!

 **IMPORTANT**

Even with a well-constructed process for ongoing success, your thoughts and emotions will either *keep you on track* toward your desired outcome or *derail you*—every time.

Reframe *Preventing to Enabling*

Your thoughts directly *help* or *hinder* your success. Although it's debilitating, it is also natural to see your limitations before you see your options. Like a laser beam, the choice is often to focus in on what you believe is *preventing* you from being or doing what you want—instead of *enabling* you.

What happens when the focus is on a limitation? You either choose to deal with it and move forward or choose to dwell on it and get stuck. Getting stuck is not a good choice. There's no positive personal payback for being stuck. Even if a personal payback is soliciting sympathy from others, that doesn't last and only annoys people eventually. And it usually requires much more of your energy than just moving ahead. You're in total control of what you choose to do, whether it's move forward or get stuck! Moving forward to achieve what you want is always better.

It never hurts to revisit this often-repeated fact: Your thoughts are your most powerful tool. What you think is what you attract . . . so visualize your thoughts as waves of energy that attract the same, or like, energy. If you put out thoughts of abundance, what you attract is abundance. It's a basic law of physics: Like attracts like.

As an example, when you give thanks for everything today, you think, speak, act, send out, and attract ideas and situations based on your having abundance. Thoughts, words, and actions focused on lack attract more evidence of lack. The law of attraction operates with no discernment between good or bad outcome; it just is.

Changing your thoughts changes your world.

Your thoughts have a powerful effect on your life. They help you protect what you cherish and facilitate changing what you don't. So it's important, when thinking of anything you want to accomplish, to ask yourself, "What do I think about my ability to succeed?" And, with this specific opportunity, "What are my dominating thoughts? Are they negative or positive?"

You can *transform* a *negative* thought into a *positive* one, and this is *essential* to keeping and attracting the life you want.

What you think of yourself and others can either *prevent* your success or *enable* you to achieve what you want, now and in the future. So it's very wise indeed to transform a negative thought to a positive thought, and you can do that with a simple technique called *reframing*.

Reframing is a highly effective mental exercise that asks you to first be aware of any disabling negative thought. Then you look at your present perspective—your present frame of negative thought—and consider putting that thought, or what is being said or done, inside a different frame, with the intention of seeing and describing it differently. To reframe and change your perspective of yourself or someone else, you may even want to challenge old thoughts or beliefs.

Reframing any negative thought into a positive thought definitely supports our emotional and mental well-being. We feel better and we even look better!

When you choose to reframe a negative thought about yourself or someone else, you have chosen to exercise your own personal power and can now reframe or change

- an obstacle into an opportunity,
- a false self-belief of limitations to one of possibilities,
- a personal insult into "Wow, is that person having a bad day!",
- a possible pipe dream into "It's possible",
- a misunderstanding into understanding,
- a mountain of a problem to a molehill,
- and much more.

For instance, if a friend or family member does something that upsets you, and you believe that that person probably meant it as a personal attack, the "probably" is your signal and opportunity to reframe the situation.

A colleague who has a particularly challenging family member has learned the value of reframing. When he's hurt by what she says or does, he remembers, "It's not me she's upset with, it's her stressful situation at work. And fortunately, it's a temporary situation." He has learned not to make a mountain out of a molehill.

Reframing should be easy, right?

Sometimes reframing is easy, and sometimes it isn't. Compare it to two people looking at the same painting; they can have two totally different perspectives on what the painter intended. And it's easy to have a lively conversation with the intention of understanding the other's perspective.

You might think that reframing a negative thought is as easy as seeing two perspectives of a painting. Not always true! We often are overly fond of our thoughts and beliefs and become a bit stubborn about replacing them with other thoughts or beliefs, even when it is to our distinct advantage to do so. Odd, isn't it?

If thoughts are going to dominate your mind, and of course they do, it's definitely to your advantage to reinforce the ones that enable and reframe the ones that prevent you from experiencing business and personal success.

The Reframing Exercise

Using the "Preventing reframed to Enabling" list, answer these questions to expose and reframe any thoughts that could prevent you from achieving an important goal or objective:

1. What do you want to accomplish that you haven't?
2. Which preventing thoughts do you need to reframe?
3. What enabling thoughts would help you achieve what you want?

Preventing	*reframed to*	Enabling
Lacking	⇒	Abundance
Fearful	⇒	Courageous
Weak	⇒	Powerful
Insecure	⇒	Confident
Not focused	⇒	Purposeful
Indecisive	⇒	Committed
Incompetent	⇒	Competent

Before you complete your own reframing exercise, let me share a personal example:

1. What do you want to accomplish that you haven't? To complete a book I had delayed for more than a year.

2. Which preventing thoughts do you need to reframe? What, am I crazy? I can't take the time off to write a book. Besides, what could I possibly say about individual success that hasn't already been said?

3. What enabling thoughts would help you achieve what you want? I've got great clients who want the SuccessMapping information and tools for their employees and would be receptive to creative scheduling for our other scheduled programs. This would give me time for a writing sabbatical. And, with today's business and economic environment, there's more need than ever for a proven how-to Success Map for individuals!

Now, use the reframing exercise to expose and reframe any thoughts that could prevent you from achieving an important goal or objective:

1. What do you want to accomplish that you haven't?

_____

_____

2. Which preventing thoughts do you need to reframe?

_____

_____

3. What enabling thoughts would help you achieve what you want?

_____

_____

How do you know when you have really reframed a preventing thought into an enabling thought? You will feel it.

Any fear or doubts that have stopped or delayed you from achieving what you want will be replaced with enthusiasm for possibilities. You'll feel the strength of the conviction of your thoughts and feelings—you'll be like a magnet attracting what you envision for yourself. And, with powerful feelings like these, there's just no place for "lack" or "nonaction" in your life.

 **IMPORTANT**

Choosing to think _enabling_ thoughts vs. _preventing_ thoughts will attract and present you with more possibilities and life options. That's the good news. The bad news is that this can be distracting. Good, but still distracting.

I was reminded of how distracting having multiple options can be when I spoke with a friend while attending a professional gathering at a Northern California space and science center. He described, in detail, how the astronomers use telescopes and laser pointers to cut through the dense fog of the evening to focus and point directly to a specific star. They are then able to identify the star, describe it, and relate the mythological story of the constellation in which it is found to the visitors in the observatory.

Like the millions of stars in the universe, your abundance of options is mind-boggling. Your possibilities are truly unlimited. That's all the reason you need to make sure that you are using your time and energy wisely! You can weed out the distractions and cut through the fog when you focus, by intention, on what you *specifically* want to achieve.

I've reframed my thoughts, but what about . . . my boss, or spouse, or colleague, or friend?

It's easy to fall into this trap: "I would do that, but he or she won't support me in what I want to do." For example: "I would go after that new job, but my boss won't go to bat for me," or ". . . but my wife/husband won't support the extra travel," or ". . . but my friends tell me this is not a good time to take risks," and so on.

If you are really intent on achieving a life dream or goal, now's a very good time to examine your "buts" and "howevers."

Check it out! How often have you thought or said, "I would, but/however, they won't . . ."? If you have applied this thought or statement to what others think about your life dream or goal, red flag! You've allowed someone else to prevent you from doing what you want to accomplish.

No doubt about it, we all have friends, family members, and colleagues who support what we want to be or do, or who don't—real or imagined. For sure, when you have others' support, life in general and being or doing what you want in particular is much easier. Those supportive individuals can be counted on to enable your actions right now. Perhaps they may not always do that for your other goals, but for what you want to achieve now, you've got their support—and that's no small matter!

 IMPORTANT

Don't forfeit the support of those who enable you, emotionally or otherwise, to pursue your objectives. Sadly, people who encourage us are often taken for granted. When people are taken for granted, they find little joy in giving or supporting, and tend to withdraw their support. So, remember to acknowledge those who choose to support you. Their support is a powerful asset in your business or personal life. Give thanks for them and to them!

Reinforce the support of your enabling network.

To reinforce and acknowledge those who support you now, ask yourself: "Who are the people in my life who are acting to enable me to do what I want to accomplish now? What might I say or do to acknowledge them and thank them for their support?"

- _____

- _____

- _____

Yes, but what to do about those doing the "preventing"?

Okay, you now have a plan to reinforce those who support you. That's easy for most of us. What's often not so easy is what to do about those we see as preventing us from moving ahead—those who set up real or perceived obstacles.

And, here's the good news: Building your Success Map helps you to win support from preventers!

The Problem-Solving Process in Step Five helps you understand and resolve potential obstacles, such as lack of support from others.

Then in Step Six you will use a tool, the Collaborative Conversation Plan, that will help you most effectively ask and get the support you need for what you next want to accomplish.

For now, the Goal Check tool in Step One helps you easily determine "How achievable is my goal? Does the real lack of support from someone important to my specific business or personal goal make achieving it more of a pipe dream than reality?"

With the Goal Check tool you will be able to score how important others' support is in achieving your desired results. You can also begin to develop actions in your Success Map to change any important preventing element to an enabling element.

Pipe Dreams Can Be Realized: The Goal Check Tool

Before you invest time, emotions, and resources on pursuing a life dream or goal, ask yourself, "Is what I want to accomplish realistic, a stretch, or a pipe dream?"

 IMPORTANT

What some would consider a pipe dream, others may have accomplished, sometimes with less "smarts," time, or money.

If you've decided on exactly what you want to accomplish next, you're ready to use the Goal Check tool to assess "How achievable is my goal or objective?"

The Goal Check analysis is not about quashing a dream or desire. Quite the contrary! Even if it looks like a pipe dream, your thoughtful analysis strengthens your ability to achieve what you want when you *identify* your specific goal and *know how to do* the following:

- Use your personal strengths.
- Minimize any potential issues.
- Challenge any "preventer" assumptions.
- Seek answers on "don't knows."

This quick yet thorough goal analysis helps you validate *or* alter, if needed, exactly what you want to accomplish—and no time or energy is wasted.

Based on your Goal Check analysis, you may decide to change your goal—take it up or down a level—or keep it just as it is. Then, with a clear vision of what is achievable at this time, and with new resolve, you are able to declare *with your intention to achieve* exactly what you want to accomplish.

As is often the case, sometimes a small change to a goal or desired outcome can give you a huge payoff. Here's an example:

Recently on a long plane ride, I discussed with a client, Mike, his intention of retiring early. To achieve this, one of his goals was to pay off his home mortgage. He wanted to accomplish this in five years. Although he didn't think this was exactly a pipe dream, he did consider it to be quite a stretch.

Before Mike focused his energy and actions on paying off his mortgage in five years, he used the Goal Check analysis to assess how achievable his goal was.

Before you check out what *you* want to achieve, let's look at Mike's Goal Check (shown on the following page). His Goal Check analysis of what he wanted to accomplish, "pay off the home mortgage in five years," resulted in a score of 38 out of a possible score of 50. Here is Mike's personal analysis:

- Accomplishing this goal helped reduce overhead, but did not fully address his postretirement cash flow concern.
- His assertive five-year payoff plan was in conflict with other family goals.
- His wife's support was important—she also had cash flow concerns.
- No additional income was going to be available for this specific goal.
- And, in light of the above, his passion for the goal was wavering.

Based on his analysis, paying off the mortgage in five years was still achievable. However, Mike's intention of supporting the family's other interests caused him to reexamine and change what he would need to accomplish to achieve his intention of retiring early.

Mike was able to check the achievability of his goal of five years and change it to "*pay off the home mortgage in eight years.*"

GOAL CHECK

(Assess how each criterion rates, low to high, on a scale of 1–5.)

What you want to accomplish: Pay off home mortgage in five years	Score each item (1–5)
Reasons for your goal: (Maximum score for below—10 points)	
1. Reduce monthly expenses prior to retirement	5
2. Cash flow to remain the same after retirement	3
Your overall ability to accomplish what you want *at this time*:	5
Compatibility with other life goals:	2
Priority of this goal relative to other goals:	3
Availability of needed skills and competencies:	5
Availability of support from others important to outcome:	3
Additional time available, if needed:	5
Additional resources accessible, if needed:	3
Your level of commitment to this outcome:	4
TOTAL SCORE: (Evaluate your score below)	38
• You're ready to go. Complete a quick check on scores of 4 and below to determine if a change is needed to ensure success.	(40–50)
• Assess your 3–4 score areas to determine if a change is needed to ensure success.	(29–39)
• Question 2–3 score areas to determine significance of low score areas to your desired outcome. If important, what change is needed to ensure success?	(0–28)

The Goal Check analysis gave Mike the tool to communicate and commit to a goal that now had family support. His and his wife's energies and actions are focused, by intention, on his retiring early.

Your Goal Check analysis: Discover how achievable your goal is, and uncover any needed changes to what you want to accomplish at this time, by completing the analysis on the following page.

Evaluate how well your goal checks out by rating each Goal Check criterion with a 1 (lowest) to 5 (highest) likelihood or value.

Your *personal analysis*: Now, write any thoughts, assumptions or "don't knows" related to your goal. *Strengths* = scores of 4–5, and *possible issues* = scores of 1–2.

• _____

_____

• _____

_____

• _____

_____

• _____

_____

• _____

_____

GOAL CHECK

(Assess how each criterion rates, low to high, on a scale of 1–5.)

What you want to accomplish:	Score each item (1–5)
Reasons for your goal: *(Maximum score for below—10 points)*	
Your overall ability to accomplish what you want *at this time*:	
Compatibility with other life goals:	
Priority of this goal relative to other goals:	
Availability of needed skills and competencies:	
Availability of support from others important to outcome:	
Additional time available, if needed:	
Additional resources accessible, if needed:	
Your level of commitment to this outcome:	
TOTAL SCORE: (Evaluate your score below)	
• You're ready to go. Complete a quick check on scores of 4 and below to determine if a change is needed to ensure success.	(40–50)
• Assess your 3–4 score areas to determine if a change is needed to ensure success.	(29–39)
• Question 2–3 score areas to determine significance of low score areas to your desired outcome. If important, what change is needed to ensure success?	(0–28)

(See Appendix Two or go to www.successmapping.com to access an additional Goal Check Worksheet.)

What you want to accomplish: *(If this has changed, record it below.)*

_____

_____

_____

_____

Congratulations **on completing your Goal Check!** You now have a clear direction on exactly what you want to accomplish and where you're headed. And you now have the beginning of a solid strategy to get there.

Hope is not a good strategy.

The *SuccessMapping* process is a solid strategy. As you move through each Step and Checkpoint, you build your Success Map—your step-by-step map to help you succeed with a business or personal dream, goal, or objective.

At the end of each *SuccessMapping* Step, the Checkpoint lets you say with confidence, "I've achieved an important milestone in accomplishing what I want!" *Take two minutes now to complete your first Step Checkpoint!*

step one
Checkpoint

(Check the box when completed.)

---

1. I am aware of and have reframed my *preventing thoughts* to *enabling thoughts*. ☐

   My personal evidence of this:

   •

   •

---

2. I have reinforced and acknowledged those people who are supporting me in achieving what I want to accomplish. ☐

---

3. I have assessed the effect of those not supporting my goal at this time and will develop actions using the tools in *SuccessMapping* to help gain their needed support. ☐

---

4. I have completed my Goal Check analysis and will use the information to develop actions in my Success Map to achieve my desired results. ☐

   My most important goal strengths that will help me to succeed are:

   •

   •

   Actions to eliminate issues or gain support are:

   •

   •

step two

The Power of You— with Intention

The purpose of Step Two in *SuccessMapping* is to help you:

- Understand how intention facilitates achievement.

- Use your intention to turn dreams and goals into reality.

- Prepare for and take charge of what can sabotage.

- Use an Intention Statement to focus your energies on achieving what you want.

- Start Your Success Map.

With intention in your heart—and heart in your intention—hopes and dreams become reality!

From Hoping to Having, through Intention

Great! You've made your decision. In Step One of your Success Map, you decided to take action on achieving an important life dream or goal. Your question now is "How do I take this off my wish list and make it a reality?"

If you're thinking and hoping, starting and stopping, what you want to accomplish, this for sure will delay the achievement of your important goals. It can also be a mental and emotional energy drain. This Step of your Success Map is your solution: No more delays or leaving your goal in limbo. Step Two ensures that your energy is focused on making your goal a reality, with no unnecessary start-stops. But before we explore the solution, let's better understand the problem.

For now, let's eliminate a couple of first-to-mind reasons why you might delay getting started on accomplishing a specific goal: not knowing how, and a lack of needed support or resources. You can set these two aside for now because they are addressed in *SuccessMapping* as you develop your Success Map.

Here's the problem to explore now: We are very busy people! Most of us are operating in overload as it is, with our plate full of demands for our time and energy. It's no wonder our goals are put on hold. Who has the time or energy to do more or achieve something different?

The key is to focus the time and energy you do have to achieve specifically what is most important for you at this time. And you have already started! In Step One you *decided* on a specific goal you want to achieve. And you reframed any thoughts that could undermine or prevent you from getting started or moving forward to attain that life dream or goal.

You then used the Goal Check in Step One to confirm, "Is this particular goal *totally achievable* just as I envisioned, or is it now obvious that some aspect of what I want to accomplish needs rethinking or altering?"

This is a good use of your time and energy, because either outcome is good to know! By validating or changing some aspect of your goal, you can now focus your energy—no start-stops—with the intention to achieve what you set out to accomplish. You are ready to *declare* your intention to achieve what you want to accomplish. This focuses the energy you need, and your thoughts, behaviors, and actions, to get the results you intended.

Your intention to achieve a specific business or personal goal gets you started and keeps you committed to the actions in your Success Map, in spite of normal life diversions and activities. No delays or start-stops!

"Sure you are—I've heard that one before."

Ever share a dream or goal with a loved one who looked at you, like, "Uh-huh, I've heard that before, here we go again." Well, that wasn't the support you were looking for!

Said or heard this before? "That's it! This time I'm *really* going to get back in shape!" Sad but true, for many the words reflect a genuine desire that somehow never makes it to genuinely effective action. Really, why is this so often the case? It's not because the desire to lose weight, look better, wear favorite clothes, or be healthy isn't compelling. It is.

Even the seduction of the feel-good thoughts of having rippled muscles or being able to slide into a slinky dress is not enough to cause us to take action to get the results we want. Unfortunately, passion and excitement for a desired outcome are not enough. If it were, more people who desire to be would be walking around looking muscle-toned and svelte.

Having a vision for your desired outcome is important, but it's just not enough. Without your intention to focus thoughts, behavior, and necessary actions to, for example, get back in shape, you can easily predict more of the same (new outfits in different sizes). Maybe the same job ten years from now, even if you know you should move ahead or out of it. Or that unfinished novel or the postponed trip to Europe or the boat that won't see water unless you do something. Now.

Success Blocker: *Lack of focus.* When your thoughts, behaviors, and actions are not laser-focused on what you want to achieve.

You are on the right track; you decided on and have declared your intention to achieve a specific goal. You see yourself achieving your desired outcome (e.g., "I'm looking and feeling good in my favorite black dress!"). Now turn that goal into reality—by focusing your energy and being committed to taking the actions you develop in your Success Map.

With intention, goals become reality.

Here's how you focus the time and energy you already have, to achieve what you want. In the Step Two Checkpoint you *declare* your intention to achieve what you want to accomplish with an *Intention Statement*.

Intention Statement: a statement that focuses your energy—your specific thoughts, behaviors, and actions needed—to achieve a goal, objective, or desired outcome.

Your Intention Statement is the real starting point of your Success Map. Your statement of what you want to accomplish keeps you energized, engaged, and focused on making the best decisions and taking the best actions. Like a personal North Star, it keeps you headed in the right direction to realize your life dream or goal.

Think of it this way: When you decide which goal to achieve, you set up a target with a big red bull's-eye. But that alone will not get you what you want if you never aim at or hit your target. There is enough nonrealized goals and targets as it is. Your Intention Statement is what keeps you at target practice with all arrows headed in the right direction. Hitting your target is much easier and quicker!

Even if your goal has all the earmarks of a pipe dream because of potential obstacles, your Intention Statement will keep you laser-focused on reaching it or, if you have to, adjusting it to changing circumstances. The outcome you desire in your career or personally will always be in sight. And that's really good news!

A path can be littered with "stumbling blocks."

Even if your path is littered with stumbling blocks, your Intention Statement enables you to keep moving forward. No one knows this better than Maria. Let me share her story with you.

Maria's story. I was invited to sit on a panel of women business owners at a leadership conference. The conference was focused on the personal and professional development of women. At this annual event, eight women in need who are returning to the workplace are selected to receive academic scholarships.

I was to be picked up at the airport by a car service along with one of the scholarship recipients, and that is how I met Maria.

It's hard to say who was more surprised when she approached the car, the driver or me. Her body was a head-to-toe kaleidoscope of tattoos.

As I got to know Maria during the conference, I understood why she was chosen to receive the conference academic scholarship. Still in her twenties, she is the mother of four children, one born while Maria was incarcerated. Her life had consisted of drugs and criminal gang activity, the tattoos chronicling her difficult past.

She said she and her uncle often discussed changing their lives but had not—and her uncle was murdered by a gang before he could act on any changes.

With that tragic event, Maria committed to changing her life and the lives of her young daughters. No more thinking or talking; *her intention to change was now irrevocable.*

Dreams and goals that had never been acted upon now were. She looked at everything she needed to do to change her life, decided on what was most important, and focused her thoughts, behaviors, and actions on achieving each goal.

With extraordinary courage, discipline, and the determination of her intention to achieve each of these major goals, she left the gang life and became drug free. Maria now has all of her children with her in one home, works full-time, volunteers in the community, and is attending an accelerated surgical technician program.

In less than one year, acting on her assertive plan, Maria has already accomplished much. The courts expunged her criminal record, she has written several compelling essays that earned her academic financial support, and she has managed to change her future.

And as Maria said, "Old limiting self-beliefs of what I can be or do are a thing of my past. The more our lives change for the better, the more energized we are to achieve new goals!"

With Maria's permission, I share her story as a most profound example of what it means to move from *thinking* to *doing*. Her intention to achieve each important life goal enabled her to maneuver through the numerous stumbling blocks and experience success. The change Maria has accomplished demonstrates the *power of intention*.

Without intention, goals are just good ideas.

You can have many life goals, but without declaring an intention about exactly where to focus energies and actions, they can all remain unfulfilled. And with each new idea of what you could or should do, your wish list just gets longer.

This was definitely true for Scott. Scott is in the fast-track leadership program for a client organization. He has numerous career options within his company as well as in his other business and family activities. You'd think, with all of his options and goals, that Scott would be making progress. He wasn't.

At the end of his busy work and family days, there was little time or energy left for Scott to pursue any other life goal or dream. Just maintaining the status quo had become his personal mantra, and time was slipping by.

In a coaching conversation with Scott, we discussed his career and family goals. Here are a few things from his wish list:

- Advance his career options: national accounts manager—business unit manager
- Leverage and enhance his professional capabilities: pursue master's degree—coach and develop others—leverage his talent for speaking and presentation skills
- Family goals: work/family life balance—support his wife's career goals—nurture their relationship—get back in shape—coach his children's soccer teams

And he had more on his list! When Scott shared everything he was doing and everything he wanted to do but wasn't doing, it was easy to see how his strategy—to hold off, make no decisions, pursue no additional responsibilities other than to maintain the status quo—might make sense. Understandable, for sure, but from a career perspective, dangerous.

Scott told me, "I feel like I've been treading water. It's time to kick off and start swimming in the direction I want my career to go. Instead of adding more to my wish list, I need to take action on one direction and get going!"

Scott shared with me that he had always had a passion and talent for coaching and developing others, in college and now in business. It had always been his intention to be in career positions that would let him use those personal strengths.

This is the work-related Intention Statement that kept Scott focused on pursuing and accepting his best business opportunities: *To be recognized and rewarded in the business community for my ability and passion for developing others to higher levels of performance.*

Even with the challenges of managing a sales team in a tough market, this intention kept him focused on overcoming those obstacles to coach and develop his team to new levels of sales performance.

Because of Scott's work, he was recognized by his company and was given the opportunity to interview for a business unit manager position. Here is Scott's Intention Statement to achieve his goal of securing that promotion: *To prepare for, pursue, and win the promotion to business unit manager.*

As it turned out, managing that particular business unit required less business travel and would help him achieve an important family goal as well: coaching his children's soccer teams. Scott developed a Success Map of best actions and used his Intention Statement to keep himself focused on pursuing and winning the management position. And, I am pleased to report, he did.

> **IMPORTANT**
>
> When you declare your intention to move forward and away from the status quo, that energy creates momentum for more success. Scott's Success Map of actions not only helped him achieve two goals, but it also brought him an unexpected new business opportunity! (More about that shortly.)

In business, if you've been in one industry for any length of time you pretty much know who the industry top performers are. Because of this, high performers like Scott are often pursued by other company departments in their companies and by other companies. If you are a manager of one of these top performers, you know how difficult it can be to keep top talent. And the tougher the business environment, the harder it is.

However, as a top performer you've got lots of career options and possibilities. You've earned it. That's the good news. The bad news? Although good for the ego, responding to a variety of career possibilities can be distracting. As dangerous as it is to coast along in the status quo when overwhelmed, it can be equally dangerous to your career to waste time and energy engaged in random interviewing for new jobs or opportunities just because you're sought after. When you choose to scatter your energy among all the requests for your talents, be cautious, because your intention to maintain "top performer" status could be jeopardized.

Be sure you know exactly what you want to accomplish in your career, and focus your energy on opportunities that support that intention. Your career intention certainly does not have to be the exact career track you are on, but it could focus on the type of work, skills, or strengths that you want to use.

Suggestion: Write an Intention Statement for using your energy wisely, such as: *My intention is to not get sidetracked with life's diversions, but to use my energies to achieve what is most important in my business and personal life.*

One way to do this is to know exactly what makes you feel good at work. Most of your life is spent there, so be sure to enjoy it. If not, it can be exhausting to be in an environment where you are not able to use or leverage a personal strength or skill.

One of Scott's personal strengths is the ability to coach and develop others. That new business opportunity that I mentioned? Large account development. Big job, big pay, but a lot of solo work with little colleague interaction and coaching opportunities. Although fun to pursue and interesting to think about, it did nothing to help him achieve his intention of developing team members.

Moral of the story: Don't interview for jobs you don't want. It's a waste of your time and energy, and you just might get them. And then regret it.

 IMPORTANT

Of course, if you are in between jobs, all bets are off! Interview as much as you can with the intention to find the best job with the best organization and get it, no regrets.

Regardless of your life situation, whether you're in the right job or in between, declare your intention for what you want to achieve in your career with an Intention Statement. Then take action and get started!

Don't Let Self-Destructive Thinking Blow Up Your Track

Using your Success Map prevents goal sabotage! As you move through each *SuccessMapping* Step and complete each Checkpoint, you are developing your Success Map!

Your Success Map becomes a solid track of best decisions and actions. And when you have accomplished those actions, you are assured of achieving what you set out to do.

But here's a heads-up! Once you decide, "Yes, I'm going to start right now. I'm ready to take the first step to get the results I want," be ready! Your *commitment* and *change-readiness* are about to be challenged.

So, prepare for and take charge of what can sabotage or blow up your track:

- Lack of commitment
- Fear of or resistance to change

With your commitment, your success.

Commitment check. If what you would like to be or do in your career or personal life is still more conversation than reality, you might want to do a quick commitment check. Your first question needs to be "Am I really committed to doing what it takes to achieve this particular goal at this time?" Your answer will let you know whether to quit thinking about it for now (or forever) and move on, or take action and get going.

You've already passed one commitment check. It happened when you completed the Step One Checkpoint. That alone was an indication of your commitment to accomplish something new or different. You thought of the various life goals and objectives you wanted to pursue, someday. And then you decided on which you wanted to achieve, right now.

You then took the time to check out "How achievable is my goal?" When you assessed your goal strengths and issues, you were then able to validate, or alter if needed, exactly what you wanted to accomplish. No lack of commitment there. These are acts of mental and emotional commitment.

Now, your Intention Statement and Success Map will help you stay focused and committed to taking the actions that will ensure your success.

The power of an Intention Statement. An Intention Statement points you and your energy in the right direction; it helps you maneuver through the daily maze of distracting choices and stay on your preferred track. Now, any normal life distraction that could shake your commitment or derail your Success Map will be obvious. Staying on track is easier when you have an Intention Statement that always keeps you focused on achieving your desired results.

As an example, let me share two of my Intention Statements. Even with enticing business and personal distractions, these Intention Statements help me to not get diverted and to stay on track to achieve both goals.

Helping others realize more of their potential is one of my life work intentions. It keeps me energized to go the extra mile and do what needs to be done in my consulting and speaking engagements to help others realize more of their potential. It has also led me to accept wonderful new opportunities and prevented me from accepting others. My Intention Statement for what I want to accomplish in my life work is: *To help others realize more of their potential.*

This life work intention clearly guides me, like my personal North Star, to know which other business or personal goals to pursue. Accomplishing those goals will then help me accomplish my life work goal.

As an example: One way to accomplish my life work intention was to write a book in order to document a step-by-step process for individual achievement. And when I achieved my goal of writing *SuccessMapping,* it would help me accomplish my intention of helping others achieve more of their potential.

So, writing *SuccessMapping* became a goal on my wish list that consumed much of my thinking and talking time. Not much action, but definitely a lot of thinking.

With no worthy-of-mention actions to chronicle my movement forward, I began to suspect, "Perhaps I'm not really ready to invest what looks to be a herculean effort of time and energy into this book project." Hmmm, delays and start-stops—it was evident that my lack of commitment was about to sabotage the achievement of my goal.

It was amazing how many reasons I had for delaying. Too much business travel, time-consuming client projects, no time for research, not the right editor, family activities, and on and on. With all the start-stops and delays, time was slipping by.

And then it occurred to me, rather late I might add, that I had not declared an intention to focus my energies and actions on completing the book! My time and energy had been committed to other business projects. Writing the book was a goal on my list that had been earmarked "someday" without my realizing it.

With the next Intention Statement, then, I focused my energies and committed to taking the actions to start and complete the first book in the *SuccessMapping* series: *My goal is to commit the time and resources for a writing sabbatical to complete* SuccessMapping *by the end of the year.*

"Someday" clues. How do you know if you've earmarked your important dream or goal for "someday"? You'll think or say comments like these: "I don't have the time now but I'll start when the business travel lightens up/ soccer season is over/the children start school/the children are through with school/I get promoted/the job feels more secure/I get married/I become single/the economy is better," and on and on. There will always be reasons, good or not, for not getting started or staying engaged. The key is to know the difference between really needing to delay a project and letting delay become a habit because of normal life diversions.

Hoping to accomplish something different without the commitment to stay engaged until you get your desired results is like pouring water into a bucket riddled with holes and expecting at some point in time to have a bucket full of water. Hugely disappointing, frustrating, and a waste of water!

With your energy focused on making change in your life, the normal life diversions will not delay or sabotage your success. Even with a momentary delay of an illness or unexpected important business or family responsibility, your intention to achieve your goal will have you quickly back on track, as soon as you can.

Even with the normal life diversions and challenges, using your Intention Statement to keep your energy focused on achieving what you want to accomplish can immediately break a start-stop habit.

Without my Intention Statement to keep me focused and committed, *SuccessMapping* would never have been completed. My ability to devote the necessary time and energy to finish the book was challenged more than a few times. But my intention to complete the book within a specific time frame kept me from getting diverted with other business and personal options. Although there were a few times when I questioned the sanity of my choices, even with the lure of profitable business and fun trips, my Intention Statement kept me on track.

Are you change-ready?

If you are willing to think, talk, or act differently when you need to be successful, no problem—you are change-ready!

If you are not prepared or comfortable with the idea of changing beliefs or behaviors when needed in order to be successful with a new business opportunity or relationship, heads up! That refusal or discomfort could easily sabotage your business or personal success.

 IMPORTANT

When you choose to do something new or different in some aspect of your life . . . there will be change. As you make progress to achieve what you want, you may find that your actions need to be altered to fit the circumstances—ah, more change! It's not a good idea to treat being change-ready as a life elective you can choose or not. It isn't optional.

To be successful in life situations, being change-ready is a much needed competency. But there's good news: Other than having to get over it—you might need to *do* something different to *have* something different—there's no downside for you when you choose to be change-ready.

Step Three and Step Eight of *SuccessMapping* provide change-ready information and tools on how to stay on track and achieve what you set out to accomplish. You will recognize the benefits and consequences of the three change choices and know how to stay engaged in what you set out to accomplish—and not fall into the trap of defaulting to the status quo. You will learn how to recognize and manage change dynamics and quickly be successful with any new or different business or personal situation.

Using the information and tools of these two Steps will populate your Success Map with the best decisions regarding the thoughts, behaviors, and actions that will help you achieve your goal.

Fear: "The Big Preventer"

We all experience some degree of fear or resistance when asked to change and do something unfamiliar or different. Even with an exciting change that we want, like a new job or relationship, when the time comes to be or do something different, resistance can set in. It's amazing how hard we make this!

The *idea* of going through change is rarely the hurdle to leap. It can be a hurdle, however (small or big is up to you), when the time for thinking is over and it's time for doing.

As an example: Let's say you've just been promoted to a new management position—congratulations! And with that promotion, you've got lots of relationship and responsibility changes. Oh, and at the same time you've just made a big commitment with an important personal relationship. All righty, more change. Feel the stress?

But you're okay—you've thought about it and you've accepted that to be successful with that hard-won management position and cherished personal relationship, you know you're going to have to make some changes. Perhaps you'll need to reassess your leadership style and ramp up on your coaching and meeting skills. And definitely it would be of value to learn how to resolve conflict quicker and communicate more effectively. That's a lot to think about, but you're up for it. Well, at least in your *mind* you are.

Experience shows us that it is sometimes easier to think about change than to actually change. What was simple in theory can be difficult, if not terrifying, when actually attempted.

Fear is a destructive emotion. Unless you're in a physical survival situation, fear serves you not. I call fear "The Big Preventer." Fear can cause us to

- not take calculated risks in our career—bad business strategy;
- not trust colleagues or team members—fine, you get to do all the work;
- not open our heart in personal relationships—well, that's not fun;
- not seize opportunities to showcase our capabilities and talents—being invisible does not help job security; and
- not be all we desire and can be.

In the not-too-distant future some of us (myself included) will realize that our fear of investing in anything during this economic climate has caused us to miss out on a smart investment. Fear helps us make prudent decisions and can also cause us to make decisions we regret. The key is to know whether a decision will help or hinder your short- and long-range objectives.

With intention, fear can be conquered.

You can formulate an intention to conquer any limiting fear. Here are some tips and techniques you can use to reframe the sensations of fear:

- Remember to breathe, *really*. Take deep, even, calming breaths.
- Think of what you are physically feeling, such as nervousness. Then focus your mind on an image of how you would like to feel—confident, calm, and strong. Repeat this until you've replaced that feeling of fear and nervousness.
- Face the fear—just do it. *Not doing* it keeps you fearful.
- Start with a little risk, then GO BIG. For example, present to your team before presenting to the executive team, or accept a minor role in a new project before taking on a leadership role.
- Mentally state your intention to reframe what you fear to a positive image, and replay it over and over in your mind before the situation. For example, "I am highly competent, and I easily and confidently communicate when doing presentations. I'm looking good!"
- Practice, practice, practice whatever new skill is needed before it is needed. Improvisation can be a risky proposition.

The more prepared you are for change, the less fear and resistance you will have. Understanding your change situation and getting the information and support for any new skill you need will help you reduce any discomfort that comes with change.

Not all discomfort is a bad thing. Discomfort can be the barometer that lets you know you've moved from the old status quo way of thinking or doing to something different. And in today's volatile and changing business environment, being change-receptive is a very good thing.

To really embrace and be comfortable with change, see yourself as eagerly stepping away from the old and slowly engaging in the unfamiliar or the new until it becomes familiar. Repeat after me: "Fear ceases to prevent me from achieving an important career or personal goal!" Then you can sigh with relief—yes, you have a new status quo!

Progress is energizing. Whether your progress forward is a small step or a huge leap, it's all energizing. Conversely, if you have little or no movement forward to achieve one goal—if you let fear hold you back—the lack of momentum can drain your energy for other important life activities. This does not have to be!

Regardless of your business or personal situation, you have been granted an "open-door policy" for life's possibility. All you have to do is open the door, step in, decide what you want, and then declare what you want to accomplish *with the intention to achieve it.* This moves you from thinking and hoping to doing and having. Even with small steps forward, it's invigorating to know that you are realizing more of your potential. It's like charging your mind and body with a high-voltage battery!

Your Intention Statement—The Power of You

Before writing your Intention Statement for what you want to accomplish, ask yourself, "Is this specific goal what I want to focus my thoughts and actions on, right now? If your answer is "No, now that I think about it, not now," then let it go. Cease to burn brain cells thinking and dreaming about it. If it's important to you, make a plan to come back to it when you are ready to take action.

If your answer is "Yes, this is exactly what I want to do right now," you are ready to write your Intention Statement to achieve what you next want to accomplish in your work or personal life.

Your Intention Statement provides you with the focus to make the best decisions and actions needed to keep you on track as you move through the *SuccessMapping* Steps and Checkpoints and develop your Success Map.

Thinking of what you next want to accomplish, you are ready to write your Intention Statement! It can be as succinct and brief as one sentence.

step two
Checkpoint

(Check the box when completed.)

Write your Intention Statement for what you want to accomplish: ☐

_____

_____

_____

_____

Start your Success Map

By completing the Step Two Checkpoint, you have taken the first step in starting your Success Map!

Go to Appendix Three and record your Intention Statement. Continue to record your best decisions and actions with each Step and Checkpoint of *SuccessMapping*. As you complete your Success Map, your Intention Statement will keep your thoughts and actions focused on achieving your specific business or personal goal.

By deciding what you want to accomplish and writing your Intention Statement, you are now ready to start your Success Map!

step three

The Power of Choice!

The purpose of Step Three in *SuccessMapping* is to help you:

- Understand how the three change response choices impact your personal success.

- Know the power of your thoughts, behaviors, and actions with each choice.

- Consciously choose the change response that moves you toward what you want!

Your Choices: Holding You Back or Moving You Forward?

When you declared, "Yes, I'm ready to achieve an important career or personal goal," you might as well have picked up a megaphone and proudly announced, "Come at me, I'm ready for change!" You may not have realized you made that loud announcement—well, actually, some people do—but for sure you've just invited change into your life. And with that intention to achieve something new, you opened the door to experience more of your life possibilities. So, don't shut the door with poor change choices before you can experience success.

If you want to achieve something new or different in your business or personal life, *please prepare yourself* for what you need to think, be, and do differently to succeed. Because how you choose to respond to change with thought, behavior, or action—small or big, easy or difficult—will determine with surprising accuracy whether you achieve what you want or you don't, as well as how easy it will be and how long it will take.

There's nothing worse than looking in your life's rearview mirror and seeing an important missed opportunity because of something you didn't do but could have done. And only now is it glaringly obvious why. It can be most distressing when reflecting on that missed opportunity to realize that if you had only done that one little thing differently, the outcome could have been exactly what you wanted!

Hate it when that happens.

Reflecting back on a missed opportunity with the perfect clarity of twenty–twenty hindsight doesn't change what was, but it can change what could be.

I'm of the school of thought that says, "Things happen for a reason, and I am content with the knowledge that all is exactly as it should be right now." Don't believe that? That's okay. For now, pretend you do. It will make you feel better!

So, instead of spending time and energy on mentally replaying the scenario of what could have been if you'd just had that one conversation, met with that one person, or taken action at that specific time, let it go, rack it up as good experience, and use that new self-knowledge to help you prepare for future change opportunities.

The choices you make, how you think and behave, and the actions you take are reliable predictors of your success. The good news: You're in charge. You are in total control of your change response choices. This preparation for what you might need to think or do differently reliably predicts how successful you will be in achieving the results you want.

The key is to not get stuck dwelling on what was or what could have been. It's to your advantage to think instead about what you want to accomplish right now; to consider the potential changes that are going to require you to think or act differently; to ramp up your skills; and to prepare your mind to go for it.

 IMPORTANT

Be aware of the impact that your decisions and choices have on all aspects of your life. *Consciously choose* those that support you in being and doing what you want, not just someday but now.

In Step One of *SuccessMapping*, you analyzed a goal and confirmed or changed it. In Step Two, you declared your intention to focus the thoughts and actions needed to achieve what you want to accomplish with your Intention Statement.

The question you will answer in Step Three is: "Are my change response choices *helping* me or *blocking* me from accomplishing my Intention Statement?"

Success Blocker: *Choosing not to engage.* Making decisions that do not help you achieve what you want. When needing to change, choosing to wait and see—and doing nothing different. Or choosing to oppose or resist engaging in the change opportunity.

You have a tremendous amount of untapped personal power to create the life you want by choosing—decision by decision—to either stifle, give away, or claim this power. How to claim and harness this power? Consciously choose thoughts and actions that *help*—not *hinder*—your ability to change what is needed to improve and progress!

The Good, the Bad, and the Ugly of Change Response Choices

Let's face it: Life is complex enough as it is. So my vote is for taking the easiest route when leaving the old way of doing something and moving to the new. Being or doing something different *does not* have to be difficult! It just has to be smart. Knowing how you respond to change helps you make smart choices to accomplish what you want more easily and more efficiently.

Studies show that when you are asked to engage in change—to be or do something different—you will respond in one of three ways:

- Engage—to move forward and take action
- Default—to do nothing, wait and see, or protect the status quo
- Oppose—to resist or move in the opposite direction

All change situations give you the opportunity to step up and claim and use your personal power. Exercise your own power by thinking about and consciously choosing the change response that brings you the best results.

Research has shown that without preparing your mind and skills to be ready for change opportunities, the majority of the time you will often choose to default by doing nothing other than protecting the status quo. Or you choose to oppose by using your energy to resist moving forward or even to move in the opposite direction. Generally, these choices do not serve you well. (Of course, if you know the change is going to be intolerable or irrational—or illegal or financially unwise—defaulting or opposing have their uses!)

For sure, if you have an intention to achieve something new or different, to engage is your best choice. Moving forward and taking action on what you need to do is what gets you the results you want.

Jumping ship is not always the best option.

If you're in a job or personal situation that doesn't seem fair to you and the environment is riddled with dissatisfaction, you have the option of changing that situation or exploring new opportunities.

If you were, say, in a rowboat with ten other people and you were doing all the rowing, and you looked back and saw half the crew doing nothing and the other half padding backwards, you'd be interested in being in any other rowboat but that one. Time to explore options and exercise caution! The fact is that any other rowboat will have its own inequities and its own inner turmoil. Every business, every relationship, is continually changing. If you make a big change, you can expect more big changes to follow.

Any organization intent on thriving in a competitive business environment is also rocking with change. Changing rowboats may result in a nice honeymoon and a short reprieve, but eventually change is going to start rocking your new boat, too. So before jumping ship, first think of the likelihood of this change situation being common for most organizations and then assess your personal and career value for engaging in the change right where you are.

You can't prevent change, nor would you want to. The world we live in is changing. Companies that are intent on surviving and thriving are attempting to maintain the same pace as the marketplace demands. From an organizational perspective, *having no change* is a loud and clear signal that you're on a sinking ship!

People grow and mature. Relationship needs then change. Organizations ride economic waves up and down. Learning, growing, and engaging in each change opportunity—that's your best protection. With change, there is only one thing to do: *Engage with it.*

✅ IMPORTANT

With any genuinely attractive change opportunity, if you choose to *wait and see* or *resist moving forward* to be or do something differently, you have chosen not to succeed. If that is the outcome you wanted, all is well.

If you want to experience a successful outcome with a particular change opportunity, choosing to engage is your *only choice*.

Your choices are transparent to others!

Most organizational changes—restructures, mergers, technology changes, new markets, and more—rarely achieve the major stakeholders' planned results. Why is that? You could argue, and rightfully so in some instances, that some business initiatives were unachievable pipe dreams in the first place. But truth be told, that's not the real problem.

Typically, a bunch of individuals are the life of these organizations, and not everyone is paddling in the same direction. Each individual is choosing to either engage in, default on, or oppose moving forward with each change opportunity. From CEO to dockworker, each individual's response—to engage in change or not—can totally derail organizational success and any individual personal gain.

When a change is announced to a group, the percentage of people who choose to engage is remarkably low. Various studies all agree that this number is right at 28 to 30 percent. With that dismally low percentage of people willing to be or do differently, it's no wonder most mergers and acquisitions fail.

Kind of makes you wonder, "What effect might my own percentage of choosing to engage (or not) in a personal change opportunity have on my relationships?" Scary thought.

And what is even scarier? You choices are transparent to others. How you respond to change situations is typically no secret to most business colleagues or family members. They hear what you say and see what you do when it comes time to be or do something different from what is familiar.

So, a very good question to ask yourself and think about is "When I am asked to be or do something different, do I engage? Or do I default on or oppose engaging in the change opportunity?"

If you choose to do nothing (default) or resist or move in the opposite direction (oppose) of a change opportunity, it has an effect. Regardless of your position on an organizational chart, your choice has a ripple effect and can permeate through and hold back the entire organization. That's the power of your change response choices!

Conversely, if you choose to *engage* and move forward, you've positioned yourself to be seen as a change leader and a high-value contributor. Plus, the group can now achieve the planned change initiative. Not always easy, but definitely always good.

When you choose to *engage* in a change with an individual or group of people, you create the opportunity for a win for them and a win for you. The term *win-win* might be overused, but when you actually achieve that business or personal dynamic, it cements relationships—and it just feels good!

Become a valued commodity. If you choose to be in that 28 to 30 percent of people who choose to be engaged and succeed with change, you will continue to differentiate yourself in areas that you need or want to succeed in. Your intention to be and stay a top performer becomes obvious to those who matter to you. You are also aware that liking the change or not is irrelevant. What is relevant is how you choose to respond.

Guaranteed job security may be a thing of the past, but enhancing job security is not. In today's economic climate, it's more important than ever to be seen in your organization and industry as a valued commodity. Having the intention to learn, grow, and be engaged in creating and responding to needed change is a must in our global business environment.

Be a valued commodity, or ride in the back of the rowboat—the choice is yours!

What if you're in a leadership role? Whether you're managing others or not, you'll shine as a natural leader when you *communicate with*, *recruit*, and *reward* teammates who get their oars in the water and paddle in the right direction. No one feels compelled to mutiny, it's easier on everyone, and you all arrive at the desired destination much faster!

What about you personally? If you're being asked to engage in a business or personal change opportunity, and it's to your benefit to do so, it's best not to stand around wishing for the old or whining about the new. A better strategy is to jump in and start paddling. It's energizing—and definitely a lot more fun!

If a discussed change, whether personal or in business, appears to be only lip service or is starting to look like smoke and mirrors, your best strategy *might be* to take the position of default and just "wait and see." But do not continue the "wait and see" strategy if the boat you want to be on is moving away from the dock! Cease to hesitate, jump in, and become an important part of the new direction.

So, when would choosing to *oppose* change be your best choice?

If a relationship or business change does not align to your career strategy, personal values, or ethics, choosing to *oppose* could be the most appropriate response for you. That boat is leaving, headed in a new direction, and you may *purposely* choose not to be in it any longer.

 **IMPORTANT**

The three change response choices also apply to a change you created, one you want and even are excited about. You may, without knowing it, be trapped in a habit of defaulting or opposing being or doing anything different. Stop it! It could cause you to miss out on a business opportunity or relationship that you really want!

Your success in all aspects of your life is constantly being affected by how you choose to respond to change, choice by choice.

To engage, default, or oppose?

Let's take two examples that illustrate the impact of the thoughts, behaviors, or actions that could accompany each choice.

1. "I've got to lose weight and get in shape."
(Scenario—You are seriously working on losing 10 pounds before a big social event. You've just been presented with a slice of your favorite, and mine, three-layered, double-fudge cake . . . and it looks scrumptious!)

Engage: "That slice of cake really looks tempting, but I'm determined to reach my ideal weight goal. So, no thanks!"

Default: "I've not had that much to eat today. A little slice couldn't hurt, and I don't want to hurt her feelings by turning it down. I'll get back on my dieting program tomorrow. Yes, I'll have a piece!"

Oppose: "It's been a terrible day. I deserve a little treat. Besides, it's a lousy time to start this dieting program. I'll start up again when there are fewer (*family, work, holiday, etc.*) activities and less stress. Sure, why not. I will have a piece!"

2. "I need to go back to school and further my education."
(Scenario—You're attending an accelerated evening program at your local university, and your first critical exam is scheduled on the same night as a concert and you have tickets that include a backstage pass and an opportunity to meet the star of the show, a personal favorite!)

Engage: You're committed to passing the class, so you decide to speak to your professor about an alternative test date. If this is not possible, you give the tickets away to your best friend, and with renewed resolve you take the test.

Default: You put off contacting your professor until the last minute. No alternative testing dates are available. Now you don't have time to give the tickets away. It's the day of your exam, and you're still in a quandary about what to do.

Oppose: Your conversation with the professor results in an argument, confirming he has something against you! It's apparent now you couldn't learn anything from someone with that attitude. Because of his reaction you decide to drop the class. He probably wouldn't have given you a passing grade anyway, even if you had earned it. There's no real reason not to go to the concert. So, sure, of course you're going to go!

Your Power of Choice

When you choose to engage in a change, your thoughts, behaviors, and actions automatically reinforce and support you moving forward to achieve your desired outcome, or alter it if you need to.

Imagine getting caught in quicksand. That's what default thoughts and behaviors do. They bog down your progress. Without even knowing it, you've allowed your mantra to become "Tomorrow, tomorrow, tomorrow." This strategy of hope without action robs you of the joy of experiencing progress today and dreams fulfilled tomorrow.

When you choose *opposing* thoughts, behaviors, or actions, the likelihood of your success with that specific change situation is minimal at best. At worst, not being or appearing to be willing to make any needed changes can damage business and personal relationships.

Prepare to make your best change response choices.

Thinking of what you want to accomplish, refer to your Intention Statement in Step One, and now complete the Power of Choice Exercise. As you move through the Steps of your Success Map, this exercise will help you make the best choices as each potential change situation or need occurs.

Exercise the Power of Choice

To realize success, you must make choices that help you engage in change and seize opportunities. To achieve your Intention Statement from the Step Two Checkpoint, here's how to prepare to make the choices that best support you:

1. Focus on what you want to accomplish with your Intention Statement.

2. Identify any potential change situations or goal-relevant opportunities you need to prepare for, and decide how you want to respond.

3. With each potential change situation or goal-relevant opportunity, identify what your behaviors would be if you chose *to engage, to default,* or *to oppose.*

POWER OF CHOICE EXERCISE EXAMPLE

1. Your Intention Statement: To effectively manage the new project team and exceed our project objectives.

2. Examples of situations or opportunities to prepare for: Different colleagues to manage, additional time at work, more business travel, reporting responsibilities to different levels of management.

3. One situation or opportunity to prepare for: Different colleagues to manage.

To *engage*: Set one-on-one meetings to determine expectations; be receptive to resolving areas of conflict; be curious about and appreciate each team member's unique ways of contributing to the achievement of project objectives.

To *default*: You're busy in meetings and travel; everyone knows what needs to done. The team meeting defined all the project timelines and who needs to do what. If there's a problem before our next meeting, they know they can call me. I'm always available.

To *oppose*: Everyone was selected because they can do the job. If someone can't do what needs to get done, I need to know now. I don't have time to babysit anyone.

With each change situation, which response helps you achieve what you want to accomplish?

_____

_____

YOUR POWER OF CHOICE EXERCISE

1. Your Intention Statement:

_____

_____

2. Examples of situations or opportunities to prepare for:

_____

_____

_____

3. One change situation opportunity to prepare for:

_____

_____

To _engage_:

_____

_____

_____

To _default_:

_____

_____

_____

To _oppose_:

_____

_____

_____

With each change situation, which response helps you achieve what you want to accomplish?

_____

_____

(See Appendix Two or go to www.successmapping.com to access an additional _Your Power of Choice_ Worksheet.)

When aware, you do choose your best change response choice!

Not being aware of the powerful effect of your choices can result in poor decisions or missed opportunities. *Being aware* of this power enables you to proactively respond with thoughts, behaviors, and actions that best represent who you are and what you want to accomplish.

 **IMPORTANT**

Depending on your specific change opportunity, there's potential personal gain in choosing to engage, default, or oppose. They are all good decisions in the appropriate cases. When thinking about responding to or making a change in your personal or business life, just consider these two questions:

Q: When is it okay to choose the behaviors of *default* or *oppose*?

A: It's *okay* when you have *consciously* evaluated the benefits *and* consequences of each response-to-change choice. If your decision to *not engage* with that change opportunity is made consciously and with confidence, then yes, that is your best choice.

Q: When is it *not* okay to choose the behaviors of *default* or oppose?

A: It's *not okay* when it has become your *habitual response* to most change situations or opportunities. If you're serious about living life abundantly and experiencing more of your potential, you must be brutally honest about your natural response to change.

Consistently stepping back from being or doing anything different is a bad habit that does not serve you well at all. It can mean making bad decisions for yourself. If that is true for you, this is your wake-up call. You can now let that debilitating habit go!

 **IMPORTANT**

You are *supremely capable* of changing any habit that blocks you from being or having more of what you value.

Next time you either initiate a change or are asked to do something different, just ask yourself, "What's the value of me being engaged—getting in the game and stepping up to bat—versus watching from the stands or not even going to the game?"

The more you show up and play, the more you strengthen the unconscious habit of seeking and participating in opportunities that are most important for you. And the added benefit to you? You become a better player and get invited to play more!

You have tremendous unclaimed personal power and human potential. Choosing to *engage* in your life opportunities is your catalyst to claim that power.

That's a habit worthy of your time and energy!

Now that you're fully aware of the power of your choices, complete the Step Three Checkpoint before you go on to Step Four of your Success Map.

(Check the box when completed.)

You know you are truly aware of the impact of your choices—thoughts, behaviors, and actions—when you *answer and check each box below*:

1. In thinking of how to achieve my Intention Statement, I have considered the potential change situations and have envisioned the thoughts, behaviors, and actions that will help me move forward with what I want to accomplish. ☐

2. With each potential change situation, I have evaluated the benefits and consequences of each of my choices *to engage, to default*, or *to oppose*. ☐

3. By consciously choosing to *engage, default*, or *oppose*, I realize I am responsible for and totally in charge of my experiences and outcomes. ☐

4. I now understand the power and potential of my choices. And that's exciting! ☐

step four

Using Your Strengths

The purpose of Step Four in *SuccessMapping* is to help you:

- Identify your strengths.

- Determine which strengths to use to achieve your Intention Statement.

- Leverage these strengths to more easily gain your desired results.

*Using a personal strength you have now to more easily achieve
what you next want to accomplish is an exercise of personal power.*

RIGHT NOW, YOU ALREADY POSSESS THE PERSONAL POWER and strengths to more easily achieve what you want to accomplish next! You've got strengths that you've learned and you've earned. Your unique skills, competencies, positive character traits, and strong values are all part of your strengths. And when called into use, those strengths can help you make good decisions, work more effectively, and live life to the fullest.

The question is, do you call on and use your personal strengths the way you could.

> **Success Blocker: *Ignoring your strengths.*** Not knowing, not utilizing, or not leveraging your personal strengths to help you more easily achieve a goal.

Some of our strengths are like old shoes tucked away in boxes in the back of our closet. In fact, sometimes you even forget they're there. Then some event or reason to wear them triggers in our mind, "Didn't I have a pair of black patent shoes that would be perfect for tonight?" The search begins through the maze of closet clutter until you find the box with the right shoes.

That's often how personal strengths are treated. You know you have personal strengths. But here's the problem: You've tucked some of them away in the closet of your mind, to be pulled out only when you remember they're there. You take them out when you need them—sometimes.

When you want to achieve something new or different, that's definitely the time to remember your strengths. The old saying "What won't break you will make you stronger" is so true. You know you have many personal strengths just by being in business and having personal relationships, so use them to help you achieve what you want more easily and efficiently.

If you don't, it's the same as forgetting you have the perfect pair of shoes in your closet and running out to shop for new ones. Who's got the time for that? Use your strengths—those skills, competencies, and character traits you've learned and earned.

You can waste a lot of time and actually jeopardize achieving a life dream or goal when you don't take the time to figure out the strengths you have and use them. Here's an example: Let's say you manage a team, and your team is responsible for a highly visible corporate project. And, meeting or exceeding the project objectives would definitely be a feather in your career cap.

Unfortunately, you've just discovered there's some conflict within your team over responsibilities. And at team meetings, there are heated discussions over who's supposed to be doing what, and when. Consequently, not much progress is being made.

You know one of your leadership strengths is the ability to communicate effectively and solve problems. Those are definitely great leadership skills! But you're busy with other work, so you choose not to get involved and use your strengths to help the team quickly resolve its issues. Instead, you decide to let the team muddle through it, duke it out, and learn how to resolve issues without your stepping in. Uh-oh.

Because you didn't realize the value of using your leadership strengths in this situation, that tight project deadline is now being jeopardized by team members squaring off in debate at each project meeting. The likely outcome? The project is not completed on time, your business goal is not realized, and, I suspect, a feather just fell out of your career cap.

If you've worked in an organization of any size, from two to thousands of people, you've seen how team dynamics can help or hurt individual and team results. In today's business environment, failing to leverage strengths to help you or your team members achieve a goal is not a smart business strategy. And it's a waste of time and energy for everyone.

Leverage Your Goal-Relevant Strengths

Here's the objective: Protect your time, energy, and desired outcomes by leveraging the strengths you have. Flex and build those muscles you have now, and gain new ones.

Step Four of *SuccessMapping* will help you identify those strengths sitting in your mental closet, so nicely tucked away and unused. You are then ready to select and use your most *goal-relevant strengths:* the personal strengths that, when utilized or leveraged, will help you achieve your Intention Statement.

Using your learned and earned goal-relevant strengths will then become something you practice unconsciously and competently. Regardless of what you next want to accomplish in your career or personal life, you will automatically ask yourself, "To achieve this goal as easily and quickly as possible, what personal strength do I possess that I can use?"

There are many different types of personal strengths—those skills and character traits that help us succeed in all aspects of our life. To make sure you take advantage of all your learned and earned strengths, your first step is to scan the Personal Strengths Inventory in this step of your Success Map and ask yourself, "On that inventory list of possible personal strengths, which of those are my personal strengths?"

Once you have identified your personal strengths, then identify which of those strengths will best help you achieve what you next want to accomplish— your goal-relevant strengths. Your next question then becomes "What decision or action can I take to best leverage each goal-relevant strength?"

Richard, a vice president of engineering, had always wanted to have his own business. He was ready *now,* not "someday," to leave the known of the corporate world for the unknown challenges and expected opportunities of being self-employed.

With that decision, he began taking the steps to ensure his success.

Richard's first step in his Success Map was to write an Intention Statement declaring exactly what he wanted to accomplish: *To own a company consisting of a small group of customer-centric minded engineers that would provide high value to all involved.*

His next step was to think about all the personal strengths anyone would need to be successful with a start-up business. After identifying all of his personal strengths on the Personal Strengths Inventory, he was then able to select the goal-relevant strengths that would best help him achieve his Intention Statement.

Richard's question, "How might I use or leverage this personal strength to help me accomplish my goal?" was then applied to each of his selected goal-relevant strengths. His goal-relevant strengths were three particular personal characteristics: *analytical, relationship-oriented,* and *resourceful.*

Richard specified the actions that would exploit or leverage the strengths he identified in his Success Map:

Analytical

- Thoroughly research the market potential for his business ideas and services.
- Make financial decisions based on analysis and facts and not on emotions.
- Weigh the criteria for hiring his engineering staff to depend less on friendship and more on needed specialized skills.

Relationship-oriented

- Leave the old organization with all relationships intact, with no burned bridges.
- Successfully recruit the key employee talent he had identified for his new business.
- Gain an agreement with his old organization to contract his engineering services in order to help them quickly respond to and secure new business.

Resourceful

- Secure agreements with his old management team to refer to him prospective business that does not meet their ideal customer profile.
- Sublet space to keep costs at a minimum for the first year of operation.
- Form alliances with vendors to share profits and reduce costs on large business opportunities.

Richard shared with me, "Even when the road got a little bumpy with the challenges of being self-employed with a young family, my Intention Statement kept me and my wife focused on why I started the business and the benefits of achieving our business goals. I can think of many times that being able to stop, think about, and identify which personal strength I needed to leverage kept us from making decisions based on fear and helped us to keep moving forward."

Richard's ability to make decisions based on logic, not emotions; to create and maintain strong business relationships; and to maximize his resources helped him achieve what he set out to accomplish with his Intention Statement.

Would he have achieved his new company business goals without intentionally leveraging his personal strengths? Yes, I think he would have. It just would have been harder and would have taken longer.

Learn how to leverage your goal-relevant strengths.

You can use or leverage the goal-relevant strengths you *know* and *have*—right now—to help you achieve your desired results easily and efficiently, in spite of bumps in your road, by using these three steps.

1. Use the Personal Strengths Inventory to identify your personal strengths. You do that by asking yourself, "Which of these personal strengths allow me to do well and enjoy what I'm doing, and are available for me to use again and again?" Your answers will let you easily identify which of the possible strengths on the inventory list are *your* personal strengths.

2. Think of your Intention Statement when using the Personal Inventory List:

   —Which of those strengths would support anyone in achieving that goal?

   —Out of those, which strengths of yours are goal-relevant strengths?

3. Identify which decisions and actions would best leverage these strengths. With each goal-relevant strength, ask yourself, "How might I leverage this personal strength to help me quickly and more easily realize my Intention Statement?"

Then put those answers in your Success Map and get started!

"Yes, I Can, Right Now!"

Without your mental commitment to thinking, "Yes, I can, right now," the "No, I can't" wins. Too often we believe more in what we *can't* do than in what we *can* do. If you're not aware of this normal but life-restricting tendency, you could rob yourself of the real value of your innate, learned, and earned strengths. You have them, so use them!

If unaware of this normal human tendency, you could end up:

- Spending more time and energy focusing on your personal or professional weaknesses (real or not) than you do on your strengths—not a good idea!

- Not communicating, showcasing, or leveraging a personal strength that would help you achieve what you want in your business or your personal life—oops, a missed opportunity!

Not using your goal-relevant strengths to help you do something new or different is like being that leaky bucket—what goes in comes right back out, with little payback for your time and energy. Can't you feel it? Not using the strengths you have to realize an important life dream or goal is a constant drip, drip, dripping of your energy.

So, use your energy wisely. Leverage the personal strengths you have to achieve what you want *now*, not "someday."

Most of us do tend to focus more on our lack rather than our abundance. That gets us nowhere in a hurry. It becomes a self-fulfilling prophecy of not being able to be or do what we desire in our lives.

So, focus on your potential for abundance. That is a self-fulfilling prophecy worth realizing!

With this focus, and using your strengths to do what you already do best to achieve your next level of success, there's no stopping you!

This I can promise: When you use goal-relevant strengths to help you be or do something different in your business or personal life, you will feel stronger and look better. Of course you will! You're coming from a place of your own personal power, and that's most attractive.

In times of need, yank those strengths out of your closet!

Sometimes it takes the wake-up punch of a life trauma for our strengths to become obvious. Most of us, at some time in our lives, have experienced a loss or trauma that almost took us down. Those experiences are not easy to weather but can give us new strengths.

That was my experience during my recovery from a major illness. Twenty years ago, I heard the dreaded words, "You have cancer and it's aggressive."

Have you ever noticed that when bad things happen, it's never at a good time?

I had just begun my speaking and consulting business, and now my new adventure included trying to survive oral cancer. Virtually abandoning my new business for the next year, I began a journey focused on my new intention of healing and surviving.

After they performed extensive surgery, doctors informed me that my speaking and singing voice would never be the same. While I felt so fortunate to be alive, the doctors' prognosis was not what I wanted to hear.

It was a dream, a vision of something I'd yearned to do—to be a cabaret singer! It's hard to admit now, but I'd always wanted to sing in a jazz club. I could hear myself telling stories and touching people's hearts with song.

Business situations competing for my time, along with a fear of the effect that career choice might have on my family, always precluded my pursuing that life dream. In looking back on that missed opportunity, I could see that there were a few personal strengths I had not thought to use, much less leverage.

Being a *problem solver* and *courageous* were strengths I had used in many business ventures but had not applied to my dream of being a singer. Now, because of the surgery, my vocal range had changed and that choice was no longer there.

 IMPORTANT

If you have a secret life dream or goal, *take action*: Create an Intention Statement to focus you in the right direction. Then identify and use the goal-relevant strengths that will help you achieve what you want, right now. "Someday" may never happen.

So, a singing career was out of reach. But even worse, I was told my speaking voice also would be raspy and not exactly pleasant. Well, that was disheartening.

Having just begun a new speaking and consulting practice, I knew this was not good news. If I had to lose something, why not my Southern drawl? No one, me included, would miss that!

Funny how life works! One seemingly small thing can just shove you over the edge. That's when you think, "I'm not taking any more. I don't care what anyone has to say. I'm taking charge of my life. I'm doing what I need to do!"

Happen to you? It's that personal tipping point. And you know when you reach it, it's time to step up and take action.

That's how it was with me. When they told me I would never again be able to open my mouth wide enough to eat a hamburger, as silly as it sounds, that's when I really lost it. That was it: time for me to take charge of my recovery!

My Intention Statement helped me keep my thoughts, decisions, and actions focused on taking charge of my recovery: *I will take charge of my recovery and live a life of healthy possibilities, not expected limitations.*

With this intention, I was ready to use the strengths that had been lying dormant to help me live a healthy life with no limitations.

And so my real journey began. I set aside my fear and the doctors' talk of limitations and let my personal strengths take over. I used my strengths of being *take-charge oriented* and *values-based* along with my *perseverance*—of can-do versus can't—and I took action. I started making decisions and taking actions to achieve my Intention Statement.

Using those strengths, I found and convinced a renowned expert to come to my rescue. Although my visits with him required much travel, the effort paid off. My speaking voice (and my Southern drawl) returned, and I've enjoyed many more hamburgers than I want to admit!

The personal strengths I needed had been yanked from my mental closet. Bottom line: By leveraging those personal strengths, along with the extraordinary support and personal strengths of loved ones, I found everything I needed to survive *and* thrive during this journey.

Many times in our lives, we are called to, and we do, marshal our personal strengths and forge ahead. If we can sound the bugle when we're in trouble, why not sound the same bugle to achieve our next success?

So, here's the plan: Identify and leverage the strengths you need to accomplish what you want, more easily and quickly. The more you flex the muscles of your personal strengths, the stronger they become. That's personal power!

Using the Personal Strengths Inventory

You may notice that the Personal Strengths Inventory does not include talents. For a talent to become realized and developed, it's necessary to apply personal strengths, like those that are listed in the inventory. Even the child piano prodigy needs passion and vision, along with discipline and practice, to become a virtuoso performer.

The Personal Strengths Inventory is a tool to help you identify your personal strengths. To easily identify them, ask yourself which of these personal strengths:

- have helped you to do well in the past;
- have been enjoyable when you used them;
- have made you want to use them again and again.

Using the Personal Strengths Inventory on the following page, check the ones you can easily identify as personal strengths.

Now that you've identified your personal strengths, it's time to decide: "Which of my strengths will help me more easily achieve what I want to accomplish with my Intention Statement?" Those are your goal-relevant strengths.

Before you use the personal strength tool (on page 75) to leverage your goal-relevant strengths, take a look at Susan's example (on page 74). Susan is a busy editor juggling multiple projects. She wanted to carve out time to become more involved in politics, in spite of her business schedule.

To help her more easily achieve that intention, she leveraged one of her personal strengths: She knew she was *resourceful*.

PERSONAL STRENGTHS INVENTORY

Personal Strength	Strength Description	Check if Yes
Action Oriented	decisive self-starter; less analysis; learn by trial and error	☐
Adaptable	change-receptive; flexible with ideas, people, and situations	☐
Analytical	data focused; objectively assess situations without emotion	☐
Coach	developer of others, with focus on their potential vs. lack	☐
Communicator	ability to speak, write, and explain with persuasive messages	☐
Courageous	brave; undertakes challenges; takes action without ambiguity	☐
Creative	conceptual thinking; new ideas, designs, actions	☐
Cooperative	seek mutual gain; intent on collaborative outcomes	☐
Deliberate	cautious; assess risks; due diligence prior to action	☐
Disciplined	structured; in control; timelines and metrics to mark progress	☐
Leader	vision for future; inspire others to achieve better and bigger	☐
Learner	pleasure in the process of gaining and applying new knowledge	☐
Organizer	arrange, conduct, and bring resources to plans or projects	☐
Perseverance	continue course of action in spite of difficulties; persistent	☐
Positive	enthusiastic; outlook of good (vs. bad) in people and situations	☐
Problem Solver	the fixer; energized by analyzing and finding solutions	☐
Relationship Oriented	social; caring of others; energized by old and new relationships	☐
Resourceful	ability to use resources wisely; avoid waste of assets	☐
Responsible	take ownership; choose to be accountable for actions	☐
Result Driven	quest for achievement and energized by accomplishments	☐
Self-Assured	confidence in own decisions, ability, and talents	☐
Strategic	analyze relevant elements, then create an actionable plan	☐
Take-Charge Oriented	assertive, risk tolerant, independent; less need for consensus	☐
Tolerant	open-minded, patient, unbiased toward others	☐
Values-Based	conscientious; values/beliefs of family, spirituality, high ethics	☐

(See Appendix Two or go to www.successmapping.com to access an additional *Personal Strengths Inventory* Worksheet.)

**EXAMPLE: USING YOUR PERSONAL STRENGTHS
TO ACHIEVE YOUR INTENTION STATEMENT**

Write Your *Intention Statement* Here: (Step Two Checkpoint)

Susan's Intention Statement: *To become more involved in politics.*

Goal-relevant strength	What thought or action would utilize or leverage this strength?
1. Resourceful	1. Hire someone to thoroughly research the cause I care about.
	2. Use my network to become involved with people who care about the same cause.
	3. Identify the key lawmakers who can make change happen.

With your Intention Statement from Step Two in mind, use the tool on the next page to list one to five *goal-relevant strengths* that would support you in achieving what you want to achieve. To utilize or leverage those strengths, identify at least one decision or action that will help you more easily achieve your Intention Statement.

USING YOUR PERSONAL STRENGTHS
TO ACHIEVE YOUR INTENTION STATEMENT

Write Your *Intention Statement* Here: (Step Two Checkpoint)

Goal-relevant strength	What thought or action would utilize or leverage this strength?

(See Appendix Two or go to www.successmapping.com to access an additional *Using Your Personal Strengths* Worksheet.)

Stay on track—or change tracks.

An added benefit: By identifying which strengths will best support you in achieving your Intention Statement, you will be able to confirm that "Yes, achieving this goal is a good use of my personal strengths. I'm on track and headed in the right direction."

Or you might find that your personal strengths, time, and resources would be better utilized in achieving a different business or personal objective. If so, that's good to know; change tracks and change your Intention Statement!

IMPORTANT

If you are in a business or personal situation that does not support you in using your personal strengths, achieving new goals could be more difficult and take longer. Seek new and different ways to gain the support you need to be able to use your strengths or, if necessary, change the situation.

Knowing your personal strengths can help you achieve—or change—a life dream.

Let me share Michael's story. An incredibly gifted art advisor, Michael is a sophisticate in his mid-30s, a Renaissance type in appearance, intellect, and life experience. When you look at and speak with Michael, it's hard to imagine him not achieving any important goal or life dream.

Michael's passion and intention in life was always to be a painter. He said, "I wanted to be not just a painter, but a great painter."

At an early age his talent was recognized by established artists. They all confirmed that, yes, he was gifted. As a teen, his talent was again assessed by the dean of a highly acclaimed art department at the university he attended, and the depth of his talent as a painter was again confirmed.

During his studies, he continued refining his talent and, from a technical perspective, became even more accomplished. Ultimately, he could replicate masterpieces. But this was not his intention as a painter. As Michael shared with me, "My gift as a painter was in reproducing other great painters' work. This was not my vision of my life work."

As he explained, "Great musicians, dancers, and writers have the talent to tell their stories and communicate their visions through their art. I began to realize that, although I was a great technical painter, I was not a painter who could express my own heart and vision on canvas. I was devastated."

While observing a friend, a highly acclaimed painter, advise other artists about how to communicate the vision of their paintings to fine art collectors, it hit him. As Michael said, "It became so obvious. I could clearly see, refine, and then communicate the vision of the paintings of emerging and established artists to others." By realizing that personal strength, he knew—with absolute certainty—that the intention for his life work had changed.

Michael's intention was now to leverage his talent of being a gifted painter and his personal strength of being a creative communicator to become a great art advisor.

So, even with resistance from those who knew his work as a painter, he recognized the value of his personal strength and changed the intention of his life work to being an art advisor. Not just an art advisor, but a *great* art advisor.

Michael is now a highly acknowledged consultant to some of the world's renowned art collectors. Using his new intention, he is indeed an internationally sought-after art advisor.

As you focus on your own personal strengths, you'll achieve new levels of business and personal success faster, and you'll be energized doing what you love to do!

You're now ready to complete the Step Four Checkpoint.

step four

Checkpoint

(Check the box when completed.)

By completing and checking each box, you will know you're ready to utilize or leverage the personal strengths you need to achieve any new life dream or goal.

1. I have completed the Personal Strengths Inventory and have identified my personal strengths.	☐
2. With my Intention Statement in mind, I have selected the goal-relevant strengths that best support achieving my desired results.	☐
3. With each goal-relevant strength, I have decided on which actions to take to more easily achieve my Intention Statement.	☐

step five

Transforming Stumbling Blocks into Stepping-Stones

The purpose of Step Five in *SuccessMapping* is to help you:

- Identify any obstacles that could prevent you from achieving your *Intention Statement*.

- Identify the real cause(s) of these obstacles.

- Determine actions needed to minimize or eliminate obstacles.

*With mind and actions set on moving forward, stumbling blocks
can be transformed into stepping-stones.*

ONE DAY YOU'RE ON TOP OF THE WORLD, emotions high, and you're feeling good. And the very next day what you wanted to be or do gets sideswiped, and you wonder what hit you! Our emotions can go up and then down with one thought or situation, or when an obstacle appears to be blocking us from achieving what we want.

It's normal and natural, but doesn't it just make you feel like a yo-yo sometimes? The key is to enjoy the ride up and stay on top longer by doing more of what got you up there in the first place. And treat the downs for what they really are: not stumbling blocks but potential stepping-stones to the discovery of something new and better.

As much as we might like to think that the problem is all "out there," there's no point in denying the fact that we are stumbling block co-creators!

Although we are often eager to claim responsibility for all of our ups, we don't always step up and claim responsibility for our downs. Unfortunately, this does nothing to help our swing back up. We might blame a potential stumbling block, like being told no by a colleague, a family member, or friend when we wanted the answer to be yes. But truth be told, we are an active partner in creating our own business and personal downs and stumbling blocks.

Even if claiming responsibility for all you are and do sounds like a bummer idea, it's not. Why not? Because what you claim is what you can change. Otherwise you are at the mercy of others to keep you on top of the world and feeling good. Well, good luck with that.

To achieve what you want in life, not to mention protecting your mental and emotional well-being, it's a much better idea to be aware of, take charge of, and do what needs to be done to minimize or eliminate any obstacle that could be a stumbling block in your path.

Really, there's no need for you to allow a little speed bump to turn into a roadblock!

Success Blocker: *Ignoring potential obstacles.* Not being prepared to see, resolve, or transform potential stumbling blocks.

We all have fears, self-doubts, and concerns that can keep us from starting or achieving something important in our lives. For some, it means stopping stone-cold. For others, that fear or concern was just what we needed to get going. Did that speed bump in *your* path get you refocused on achieving your goal—get you motivated and ready to charge ahead?

Even if a specific business or personal situation has all the makings of a major roadblock preventing your success, see it and treat it for what it is: a mere stumbling block to either move around, resolve, or leverage into a new opportunity.

The good news? Even with a significant life obstacle, you can minimize, mitigate, eliminate, or even transform it with the right thinking and actions. You have the tools you need with the Steps and Checkpoints of *SuccessMapping.* They provide the navigation you need to move forward in spite of stumbling blocks.

Your first tool to "prevent what can prevent you" is found in Step Two: your Intention Statement. Regardless of any speed bumps in your path, your Intention Statement will keep your thoughts and actions focused on what you want to accomplish instead of what you can't do—regardless of the speed bumps!

Step Five of your Success Map will flush out any unresolved obstacles that could block you from being or having what you want. The Problem-Solving Process is your guide to resolving a potential stumbling block and discovering new business and personal opportunities.

In this step of your Success Map, you will explore and utilize these basic premises for resolving a stumbling block or transforming it into a stepping-stone:

- Remember to treat your Intention Statement as your personal North Star. If you find yourself spending more time thinking of what could *prevent* you from accomplishing what you want to be or do, refocus your thoughts and actions on the benefits you will *gain* when you achieve your Intention Statement.

- Be willing to self-investigate. Whatever is preventing you from moving forward, know and resolve the *real cause* of the obstacle. Use the Problem-Solving Process to prevent a potential stumbling block from becoming a roadblock.

- When using the Problem-Solving Process, leverage those new ideas and actions to uncover and develop different business opportunities and strengthen relationships.

 IMPORTANT

As you take actions to achieve one goal, set aside any other potential life obstacle if it's not relevant to your specific goal. Your *sole focus* is to resolve any stumbling block(s) that could prevent you from achieving what you want to be or do right now.

With your Intention Statement in mind, focus on understanding and resolving any goal-relevant stumbling block that could slow you down—or stop you cold.

Here's an example: Let's say you have a fear of heights; this fear could very well prevent you from mountain climbing or taking flying lessons. If, on the other hand, your intention is to fulfill a lifelong dream of mastering a foreign language, your fear of heights is not an obstacle to focus on now. This fear could cause your stomach to churn when thinking of living on the top floor of a high-rise building, but it will not prevent you from learning a new language. It's not a stumbling block for what you now want to accomplish.

If, however, you really want to fly an airplane, then your fear of heights would definitely count as a stumbling block that needs to be minimized or eliminated to achieve what you want. Combine that with a spouse who has strongly expressed, "No way, this is not going to happen!"—and you may never see the inside of a cockpit.

Stay focused on seeing, taking charge of, and resolving any stumbling block, fears, or concerns that could prevent you from achieving your Intention Statement. When you do, the sky can be yours!

Your Stumbling Blocks: What They Really Are

Have you ever spent time and energy fixing the wrong problem? Most of us have, and it's frustrating! So, how would you know if you have fallen into this counterproductive trap?

Here's how you will know: It will become most evident when you've taken care of the obvious *external* obstacles—such as lack of time, money, and support from others—and still, you've not taken any action or you've delayed moving forward to achieve your Intention Statement. It's like being stuck in one spot, twirling around. It's exhausting and a time-killer. So, quit twirling, resolve the real obstacle, and move on.

My friend Nancy wanted to return to school to improve her career opportunities. With family responsibilities, she had the normal obstacles to manage. At the top of her list was not having the money to pay for school and child care when her spouse traveled. She did resolve the money and child care issues, but she still did not register for school! Uh-oh. Notice the twirling?

Even after resolving her obvious *external* obstacles, still Nancy took no steps to move forward. *Thinking* about going to school doesn't count. That's mental twirling. *Going* is what counts!

> **External obstacles:** Other people or situations that affect what you want to be or do.
>
> **Internal obstacles:** Your own fears, self-doubts, concerns, or interactions with others that prevent you from being or having more of life's possibilities.

So, why did Nancy delay taking action? She shared with me that she had not uncovered or dealt with her real obstacle—the *internal* obstacle that became evident when she asked herself, "If I go back to school right now, what am I afraid might happen? What other concerns are keeping me from going back to school?"

After her honest self-investigation, she realized what her real obstacles were. Yes, she had concerns with the additional money needed for school and extra child care. But that was not her real stumbling block. She discovered what was really preventing her from registering for school were her personal fears of

- not being available for her family when needed, and
- starting over at her age and not succeeding.

If you knew Nancy, you'd know she is a caregiver in every sense of the word. Her family had always been her priority, to the point of not pursuing any personal life dreams. So, it would have been obvious to you what was preventing her from taking action on a life dream. It just wasn't obvious to her.

It is unfortunate but true that our personal fears or self-doubts, so nicely tucked away, are usually the last place we investigate.

Armed with her new knowledge from her self-investigation, Nancy stopped twirling—no more yearning and talking about going back to school. After realizing that the real stumbling blocks between her and a life dream were her own personal fears, she stepped into her personal power, took charge, and claimed responsibility for her delays—and then she took action.

After conversations with family and a school counselor, Nancy put together an online curriculum that resolved both of her concerns. And she has experienced much success since that first semester in school. After graduating magna cum laude, she has written four books and is now excited about achieving her next success!

As Nancy shared with me, "Each stumbling block along the way gave me the opportunity to learn and grow in ways I never imagined."

One stumbling block can mask another.

Different ideas, creative options, and new opportunities and relationships "suddenly" appear when you have a mind-set for problem solving.

When you choose to accept the role of self-investigator and problem solver, everything that gets in the way of your achievement becomes something to explore, something in which you can discover new and different ways to succeed. Instead of being worrisome, it becomes interesting!

You are then able not only to resolve and transform the obvious external cause for the stumbling block, but also to delve deeper to uncover any internal fear or self-doubt that could be driving the decisions you're making and the actions you are or are not taking.

Here's an example: Let's say you are the owner of a start-up business in which you've invested your life savings. Because of the first year's unforeseen costs, you are precariously close to running out of funds. No doubt about it: Since you started your business, you've had many opportunities to exercise your problem-solving skills. Now those skills are really being put to the test.

You've considered your options for new funding, and you've seen them all before: delay business expansion ideas, attempt to sell the business, find new investment funds, or take on a business partner. The good news is that you've been approached by someone who has offered to buy into the company and is interested in being your business partner. In fact, in the last six months, you've actually had not one but two interested potential business partners. But you decided, rather quickly, that neither individual was a good business partner candidate. Or were they?

For sure, finding a good business partner fit can be as dicey as finding a good marriage fit. When you've been blessed with "good" in either of those relationships, it's like all the stars align, the heavens part, and light shines down on both of you at the same time. (Well, perhaps I exaggerate.)

So, here's your real question: Why didn't you seriously consider either of the business partners? With a little self-investigation, hastened by depleting funds, you realize that the real cause was less about the candidates and more about your fears of having a business partner—any business partner. Your key fears were:

- Loss of full ownership
- Loss of freedom to shape the company's direction
- Conflicting business goals and values

Now, with an understanding of how your internal fears have been driving your business decisions, you're in a much better position to address the fears and move on. Now you're ready to reevaluate your options and make the best decisions for bringing in funding—with a business partner or through another business option.

 IMPORTANT

When resisting a solution that would resolve a stumbling block, check it out with this question: "Is this solution really not a viable option, or am I masking this solution with another obstacle, such as an internal fear or self-doubt?

Turning Problem-Solving Skills into Personal Strengths

How will you know when you've become a problem solver extraordinaire?

- You will not allow fear, self-doubt, or concerns to prevent you from achieving something new or different in your life.
- You will not deny or delay exploring any underlying internal obstacle that could become a stumbling block.
- Even with significant obstacles, your intention to be successful will be evident in all areas of your life. You'll be open not only to resolving obstacles but also to expanding your problem-solving thoughts to explore new and different business and personal opportunities.

You'll know that problem-solving skills can be counted among your personal strengths when resolving obstacles becomes easier and requires less effort. Just like shifting gears in a car, your focus and actions will be automatic. You'll see your obstacles for what they really are, effectively resolve them, pick up new learning, and keep moving in the direction you want to go.

In business it's a must, and in your personal life you've got to have it!

The more you sharpen your problem-solving skills, the easier your life becomes. Your personal relationships run more smoothly and become stronger instead of being worn down by conflict. Your business relationships become supportive instead of divisive, your meetings are more productive, and potential issues that could affect your career gets resolved faster and more easily.

Yes, claiming your problem-solving skills as one of your strengths is a very good thing!

Ever think back with regret over a conversation that you would dearly like to redo? Unless you've lived the life of a hermit, I suspect your answer to that question is *yes*. Haven't we all? Perhaps more often than we would like to admit!

It's not because we are not kind, caring people; we are. That's not what gets us into hot water with people. More often than not, in the heat of the conversation, we react and say and do things without being understood or understanding, and the water starts bubbling. This does not have to be. Pausing in your conversations before reacting, then using the Problem-Solving Process, will keep a molehill of a misunderstanding from turning into a proverbial mountain of conflict.

Without a doubt, in business today you cannot afford to jeopardize your career opportunities by getting stuck in issues and failing to resolve obstacles quickly. Being a problem solver extraordinaire is not just an asset; it has become a career requirement.

Sam, president of a global performance organization, recently shared his thoughts on the key personal traits and characteristics needed to succeed in today's global environment.

At the top of Sam's list were *patience* and *courage.* "When we interview for new talent, we look for specific leadership qualities," he said. "We continue to succeed in the marketplace by hiring and retaining key employees who are so focused on the goal that when they take two steps forward but then take one step back, they still persist. They must have the patience and skills to problem solve and the courage to keep moving forward."

As Sam said, "Being an effective problem solver is a personal strength essential in today's turbulent business environment."

The Problem-Solving Process

The *SuccessMapping* Problem-Solving Process is simple by design, yet powerful in outcome.

Regardless of how complex your obstacle may appear, step back and see that potential stumbling block for what it really is: *just a problem to resolve and transform.*

Whether your obstacle looks like a speed bump that's easy to maneuver around or a roadblock where no progress seems possible, you can rely on the Problem-Solving Process.

This process will do one of two things: resolve your obstacle and allow you to keep moving or, based on the new knowledge gained, allow you to make clear decisions—one of which may be to change directions in terms of what you want to accomplish, declare your intention to achieve a new goal, and move forward.

It's always to your advantage to strengthen your problem-solving skills. If you're thinking, "Right, I do enough of that already," it might be a good time to do a wee bit of self-investigation and ask yourself, "Am I just involved in a lot of conflict situations, or am I known for being a problem solver?"

As Sam confirmed, being known for having problem-solving skills as your personal strength is a leadership skill worth developing. And the good news: Being a problem solver extraordinaire is a *learned* skill.

Essential in learning this skill is to (a) think like an investigator, and (b) develop a gut-level determination to uncover "the whole truth and nothing but the truth."

The four steps of the Problem-Solving Process will flush out and resolve whatever can delay or stop you cold. Thinking of what you want to achieve, ask yourself the following questions:

1. Is there an obstacle that could prevent me from achieving my Intention Statement? If so, what is it?

2. What might be the *real* cause of this obstacle?

—Is it an *external* cause . . . lack of time, money, or support from others?

—Is it an *internal* cause . . . a personal fear, self-doubt, or concern?

3. What would resolve or transform this obstacle?

—What new attitudes, ideas, behaviors, or actions would I be demonstrating?

—In resolving one obstacle, what new opportunities or relationships can be developed?

4. Out of all possible actions, which action would best resolve and has the potential to transform the *real* obstacle into an opportunity?

All obstacles are not created equal!

You'll get no argument from me—some obstacles are easier to manage than others. Sometimes our greatest gifts come from resolving difficult and challenging life obstacles. But too often, without a way to quickly and effectively resolve difficult obstacles, we simply don't try. In my business and even with family and friends, I often hear comments that loudly communicate, "This is hard. I give up. I'll let this life dream or goal fall by the wayside."

Whether you've heard this type of statement before or even said it, it's what I call a *goal-death alert*!

Here are just a few of the goal-death alerts I've heard recently:

- "I've managed to survive this last reorganization, but I can't possibly succeed with this project."

- "I really want to pursue this sales management position, but my spouse will not support me because of the extra travel."

- "I would enroll in that leadership program, but I don't have the time now."

- "I need to rethink asking for that promotion because the timing may not be quite right."

IMPORTANT

Before you send out a goal-death alert and abandon a business goal or a life dream because of a potential obstacle, reconsider. Instead, consider abandoning how you usually think and react to challenging obstacles.

Using the Problem-Solving Process gives you the steps to understand and resolve complex problems and obstacles simply and effectively.

Resolving and Transforming a Stumbling Block

Thinking of what you want to achieve, let's review and then complete each step of the Problem-Solving Process to resolve and transform one of your potential stumbling blocks.

The first step of the Problem-Solving Process is designed to help you identify any potential obstacle that could block you from accomplishing what you next want to achieve. Before attempting to understand the underlying cause of one known obstacle, take a moment to flush out and identify all potential obstacles.

Step 1. Is there an obstacle that could prevent me from achieving my Intention Statement? If so, what is it?

_____

_____

_____

The second step of the Problem-Solving Process begins with another question:

Step 2. What might be the real cause of this obstacle?

Early in my career, I retained a problem-solving guru to help me sharpen my problem-solving skills and invited colleagues to join me in the process. We were instructed to bring a business problem to our two-day meeting. Okay by me—I had a few packed and ready to go!

By the middle of day two, I was *really* frustrated. Having interesting business discussions with interesting people was fun, but we were still discussing how to understand the problem, with no conversation on how to fix it. Where were the how-to's, the techniques to resolve the problem, the best practices? Where was the concrete process to fix problems and move on?

With all due respect I approached our problem-solving expert with my concern. Being the guru that he was, he calmly informed me, "You can't fix what you don't understand."

Ah, words of wisdom. Suddenly, I got it!

 **IMPORTANT**

When you take time to *truly* understand the *real* cause of an obstacle, resolving it becomes so much easier.

So, to prevent wasting your time and energy fixing the wrong problem, investigate and answer the questions below to flush out and uncover the real cause of any unresolved obstacles:

- What might be any *external* obstacles—such as additional resource needs, like time, money, or other support?

  _____

  _____

- Who do I need to support me?

  _____

  _____

- Why would this individual or group help? Why not?

_____

_____

_____

- When the potential external obstacles have been resolved, are there any internal obstacles—such as personal fears, self-doubts, or concerns—that could still prevent me from taking action?

_____

_____

_____

- What concerns me the most about failing—or succeeding—with my Intention Statement?

_____

_____

_____

Step 3: What would resolve this obstacle?
Who better than you to know and explore all your options and resources?

Here's good news: You've already started your exploration! In the last chapter, you identified which of your personal strengths you want to utilize and leverage to more easily achieve the goals in your Intention Statement. That Step in your Success Map helped you laser-focus on *what you can do.*

Using your personal strengths and having that *can-do* focus enables you to eliminate obstacles that previously may have stopped you from succeeding with this or other goals or objectives.

Once you've flushed out and understand the cause of any potential stumbling block, then let the mind wander. Before quickly acting on an idea, stop and think, "I do not have to jump on the first possible solution. *Being* or *having* something different in my life most likely—in fact, most assuredly—requires me to be *doing* something different!"

Give yourself permission to take the time to brainstorm—with no censoring—new ideas, attitudes, or actions that could minimize or eliminate your obstacle and allow different opportunities to surface.

This is the time to expand your thinking on what you can do to resolve an obstacle. Be aware of any thoughts about why it can't work and reframe them to why it *can* work. (Refer to your exercise in Step One to review how to reframe preventing thoughts into enabling thoughts.)

After identifying the underlying cause—your *real* obstacle—give yourself the time to explore options before taking action.

Brainstorm and create a list of all possible new attitudes, ideas, behaviors, or actions that could resolve your obstacle. This is about placing no limits on your possibilities; they should range from the "for sure" to the "wildly unlikely."

Bonus: This process of idea generation often uncovers new opportunities or resources—those stepping-stones that are often uncovered when brainstorming. So "go big" and create a robust list of what you could do to resolve your obstacle.

Your real *external* or *internal* obstacle(s) to resolve:

_____

_____

_____

Possible new attitudes, behaviors, ideas, or actions:

- _____   - _____

- _____   - _____

- _____   - _____

Step 4. Out of all possible actions, which action would best resolve and has the potential to transform the *real* obstacle into an opportunity?

Best action(s):

- _____ • _____

- _____ • _____

Why are these considered the best?

_____

_____

Creating Stepping-Stones

How? You've already started! When you use the Problem-Solving Process, you've already begun to uncover different ways—*stepping-stones*—to help you not only achieve what you want to accomplish with your Intention Statement, but also discover new resources and areas of support for future goals.

What are stepping-stones? They're expanded ways of thinking about yourself and others; they're new opportunities, new levels of support, different and stronger relationships, or different paths to needed resources.

Just think: How often has a life detour or bump in the road brought you an unforeseen relationship or different opportunity? This is exactly what happened to Josh, a senior group leader in a client organization going through a massive downsizing that required shutting down its manufacturing facility. Josh and most of his coworkers were about to be displaced and were in career limbo.

Josh shared with me, "Even more difficult than coping with my own fears was helping others deal with their fears of having no job and no prospects in a tough market. Every day was an emotional roller-coaster!"

Instead of waiting for the inevitable facility shutdown, Josh took the attitude of "there must be a pony in here somewhere." He rallied the team members who were willing to make changes and planned their campaign to actively pursue other positions in business units that had not been affected by the company's downsizing.

Not only did Josh's coaching on how to be more marketable in other areas of the company secure new jobs for some of his team members, but his leadership skills also caught the attention of the corporate executives. The outcome? Josh is now happily ensconced in corporate headquarters, heading up a new business unit. Josh used his personal strengths of problem-solving and leadership skills and turned a career stumbling block into a very significant stepping-stone.

When you use the Problem-Solving Process, obstacles frequently transform into stepping-stones that often offer surprising and beneficial opportunities.

. . .

When pushing through obstacles to accomplish something new, your personal comfort can swing like a pendulum. The more unknowns and changes in your business or personal life, the stronger the tendency to hold back on being or doing anything different. If in response you become cautious, or vulnerable to push-back from others' on what you want to accomplish, you run the risk of allowing your dreams and goals to be put on hold.

During times of ambiguity in your business environment, it might seem to make sense to move through life with one foot hovering over the brake, more prepared to stop than to move forward. Here's what it might look like: Choosing not to stand up in meetings for what's not working, or not to ask for the promotion because of the complex testing and interviewing process, or not to submit ideas and take charge of new projects. Although those decisions may feel like a safe strategy, having your foot on the brake may not be your best career strategy.

Or conversely, with little regard for what's going on in your business environment and how it's affecting others, you may have your foot firmly pressed down on the accelerator, full speed ahead and paying little attention to any roadblocks. Your personal motto would be "Crash through at all costs."

Neither of these approaches will help you transform business or personal stumbling blocks into stepping-stones.

The Problem-Solving Process lets you know, "Yes, I can take my foot off the brake so I can move forward with my life." Or, "No, I do need to put my foot on the brake and reassess whether this the right time with the right people to move forward to achieve my life dream or goal."

Nancy used the Problem-Solving Process (shown below) to resolve her obstacles and move forward with her life dream.

Even if you're a high achiever, you can get into overload!

When using this process, you may find that what you want to accomplish does not outweigh what it would take—from you or other resources—to really fix a specific goal obstacle.

This is very good to know!

One of my clients, Carlos, was expanding his business to the South American market. As we discussed his plans for product development and

---

SAMPLE PROBLEM-SOLVING PROCESS

Nancy's Intention Statement: To go back to school to expand my career opportunities.

Obstacle(s):	Real Cause:	Possible Actions:	Best Action:
Not registering for school	Not being available for my family Fear of starting over at my age and not succeeding	Delay my education Communicate my concerns with the family Hire tutors for my children Change my career focus Seek school counsel	Start with an online curriculum to help me and the family become accustomed to me going back to school

implementation, our conversation often turned to another personal objective he was passionate about. Although he was traveling extensively and attempting to make more time for his young family, he also wanted to return to school to get his doctorate.

Carlos, who was comfortable with taking risks and juggling multiple projects, found huge value in using the Problem-Solving Process to weigh the importance of each goal by asking, "If pursued right now, could this jeopardize my success with other equally important life priorities?"

Even though it was evident to Carlos that he did not have the time to pursue a doctorate, he was letting his thoughts rob him of being fully engaged with what was more important to him at the time: supporting his family and expanding his business.

However, he did not totally abandon his intention to pursue his doctorate degree. He made the decision to revisit in 18 months his academic goal of enrolling in the university and beginning his doctorate program.

What did that really do for Carlos? His thoughts and actions became totally focused on being and having what mattered most to him right now. No time or energy was wasted on dreaming and hoping. He now could take advantage of living in the present!

Like Carlos, by objectively assessing a potential obstacle, you may decide, "I'm spread too thin. I would be better off waiting to start this project—setting a different time—or changing what I originally set out to accomplish."

By using the Problem-Solving Process tool and the Decision Matrix in Step Seven, you will be able to consciously—and with no regrets—evaluate your options and make the best possible decision. The real cause of your obstacle will be resolved as you move forward to achieve what you next want to accomplish.

You are now ready to complete your Step Five Checkpoint, using the Problem-Solving Process to resolve any obstacle(s) that could prevent you from achieving your Intention Statement.

step
five
Checkpoint

(Check the box when completed.)

PROBLEM-SOLVING PROCESS			☐

Write Your Intention Statement:

Obstacle(s):	Real Cause:	Possible Actions:	Best Action:

(See Appendix Two or go to www.successmapping.com to access an additional *Problem-Solving Process* Worksheet.)

Comment for the high achievers: High achievers love the excitement of the hunt and can be energized with having multiple new ideas and projects all going at the same time. That's a wonderful trait for those who can pull it off and achieve all of their expected outcomes.

The value of the Problem-Solving Process is to let you objectively look at what is really required of you to resolve potential obstacles with multiple projects. Then, at that point, you're juggling, quickly resolving any potential issues, and catching all the balls!

step
six

Ask For and Get
What You Need

The purpose of Step Six in *SuccessMapping* is to help you:

- Understand why you *resist asking*—and why they *resist giving*.

- Identify *exactly* what support or resources you need to accomplish each action to achieve your Intention Statement.

- Know how to ask for what you need . . . *and get it*.

If you don't ask, don't be surprised when you get nothing!

EVER NOTICE THAT SOME PEOPLE JUST SEEM to have the knack for getting what they want? They know what they want, they ask for it, and more often than not, they get it. One might even think these people are gifted at birth with this talent of asking and receiving! Not true.

To give credit where credit is due, some people do seem to have that special way about them—you know, that charming demeanor that emanates an aura of, "Of course you want to support me, this is a wonderful thing I'm doing, and I deserve it." Although that might not work all the time, there's a lot to be said for the value of being confident. You've got to admit that's a much more powerful approach than "I know this will be difficult for you, but I really need your help."

When you use this approach you can almost see their thoughts twirling: "Uh-oh, she wants me to do something to help her out. I'm already overloaded with my own work!" Before they even know what kind of support you need and whether it will be easy or not to provide, their mind is saying *no*. So, when asking others for support, you might want to think about your natural approach before you begin your conversation.

Whether you consider your approach charming or not, what is always most important when asking others for support is *how you communicate* and *how you manage the conversation*. And that has little to do with having or not having a charming personality.

In fact, we endear ourselves and more easily gain other people's respect and support when, before ever asking for their support or resources, we first understand and speak to their needs and situation. It's a collaborative approach. Of course, no one is saying you can't be charming, too!

Some of us naturally seek to have collaborative conversations by asking and listening in order to better understand others. And some of us have the tendency to tell and explain with the intent to be understood. If you're lucky, you do both well and at the right time in your conversations.

If you're not "lucky" in conversations—meaning you don't always get the extra time, money, or support you need to be and do what you want—it's time to consider a change! You might want to look at how you plan and how you engage in your important conversations.

> **Success Blocker:** *Going it alone.* Not using a collaborative approach to ask for and get the specific support you need to achieve your business or personal goal.

If you want to improve the outcomes of your conversations, the Collaborative Conversation Plan in Step Six will do that! You may not get what you want 100 percent of the time. Not even the best negotiators do. But you will gain more agreements than ever before and have conversations that strengthen, not weaken, your relationships.

Using the steps of the Problem-Solving Process in Step Five helped you uncover and resolve an obstacle, a potential stumbling block that could have prevented you from achieving what you set out to accomplish with your Intention Statement.

If you found out that to resolve an obstacle or accomplish an action in your Success Map you need additional resources or support from others, the Collaborative Conversation Plan will help you plan for and most effectively ask for what you need.

Effective Communication—The Collaborative Approach

You know you should be a good listener and keep the other guy's interests in mind, but in your conversations do you neglect to do it—to really understand others, their needs, and their situation before attempting to be understood and to explain *your* needs and situation? Can you imagine how healthy and strong your business and personal relationships would be if you put such a collaborative approach into practice more often? It's an amazing thought!

From resolving personal issues with colleagues, friends, or family members to negotiating complex business situations, the more you use this approach, the better the outcome of your conversations.

Your odds of having conversations that have successful outcomes dramatically improve when you have an *intention* and *focus* for

- planning and using the skills of a collaborative communicator, and
- gaining agreements and achieving mutually beneficial outcomes.

Your sole focus in this Step of your Success Map is to help you prepare for and hold conversations that will gain the support you need for each decision or action required to achieve your Intention Statement.

Before you use the Collaborative Conversation Plan to prepare for an important conversation, let's make sure you know the specifics of what you need and who's the best person or group to ask. So, with each action you have planned in your Success Map to achieve your Intention Statement, you will want to consider the following:

- What specific support or additional resources do I need to accomplish that action?
- Who is the best individual or group to provide that support?
- What is the best environment for the conversation (when and where)?

Before you decide on what to ask for and whom to ask, let's look at Josh's situation, discussed near the end of Step Five. When his company shut down its manufacturing facility, he became focused on moving fast and not waiting until the doors closed before finding a new position.

Josh's Intention Statement: To help me and my team members find new positions in this organization as quickly as possible.

Below are just two actions that he took to help him to achieve that intention.

Action	Support Needed	Who Can Best Help	When and Where to Ask
Broadcast team members' resumes to other business units	Approval and support from the corporate office	Corporate VP of Human Resources	Conference call before the next team meeting
Pursue a management position with another business unit	Executive recommendations	The present VP of Operations and the SVP of the other business unit	Before the next management meeting and at corporate offices

Josh was focused on having collaborative conversations. He knew what he needed to do, the support he needed, and whom to ask for the support, and he knew the needs and objectives of each person in his conversations. He was prepared. Now he was ready to ask for and gain agreements for what he needed to accomplish—two major actions in his Success Map. Each action, when accomplished, helped him to achieve his Intention Statement.

You might ask why it is important to take the time to do this. Yes, it may seem like a basic thought process, but it's always smart to rethink and confirm, "Am I asking the right person at the right time to get the support I need to achieve my Intention Statement?"

To make sure you're talking to the right people about the right thing, complete the box on the following page before you plan that next important conversation.

Action	Support Needed	Who Can Best Help	When and Where to Ask

To achieve your Intention Statement, you may need to take one action or several. Identify and resolve any potential obstacle, determine what support you will need and whom to ask for it, then prepare for and hold collaborative conversations to ask and get the additional support or resources you need.

YES or NO—It's good to know!

☑ They say YES—great. Cease to hesitate; get started and move forward.

☑ They say NO—the sooner you know the better. NO is not a show stopper. It's only a course redirection.

NO? Either change what you're asking for or change whom you're asking for it. If the idea of being told *no* is stopping you from asking someone for financial, emotional, or physical support, think about it: What's the worst thing that can happen? That person might say no. If so, fine. That's not exactly what you wanted to hear, but now you are free to let that resource go for the moment and concentrate on new and different resources to help you achieve what you want. And that *no* that looks like a stumbling block? It could very well be a stepping-stone to a new and exciting opportunity.

IMPORTANT

New resources and opportunities are often the result of someone telling you *no*.

Being open to thinking that a *no* answer might be a good thing is definitely a positive mental shift. This mental shift—from the negative thought "It's a stumbling block that can prevent me from achieving what I want" to the positive "It might be a stepping-stone to something new or better"— gives you all the momentum you need to move forward.

Visualize yourself throwing a magical cape of optimism and fearlessness over your shoulders and asking for what you need. *No one will know you have your fearless cape on, they can't see it.*

 IMPORTANT

Being fearless should not be confused with being reckless. So, how to know the difference? This is most important for you to know, especially if you have questions or self-doubts about how achievable your goal really is or if you're asking for a huge investment of someone's time or money.

Here's how to make certain that you're not being reckless: Review or complete the Checkpoints of Step One through Step Five of your Success Map. When you complete the Checkpoints, you've done the analysis you need to make the best decisions with the best actions. You can then feel confident, not reckless, when you ask others for the support you need.

No crawdaddin'!

To achieve your Intention Statement, *crawdaddin*'—backing away from asking for the additional support you need—does not work!

There is no place for crawdaddin' in your Success Map. If you need additional support or resources, now is not the time to get squeamish. Don't try to go it alone if you need support, don't go into default mode and do nothing, and never back away instead of moving forward. Your window of opportunity is open *now*. With your Success Map in hand and with passion in your heart, go for it!

If you don't ask, you get what you get!

Yes, you know, but it's worth repeating: If you don't ask for what you need from others, don't be surprised with what you get. And that is likely to be only disappointment or anger when your expectations are not met.

 IMPORTANT

Hard to believe, but we often expect people to read our minds, to know intuitively what we want and need. You know you do this!

Do you find yourself thinking, sometimes in anguish, "Can't they tell? Don't they know?" Red flag! Ninety-nine percent of the time, the answer would be "no"! No, they can't read your mind. No, they don't know what you need to achieve what you want. So, in the absence of letting them hear very specifically what you need, what you get is subject to their ability to read your mind. Good luck with that!

It's easier on your mind and your emotions to just take charge of what and how you communicate. First, when asking others for support, be mindful of their business or personal situation. Then, be clear on exactly what you're asking and why you're asking it. Simple in theory, powerful in outcome—and oddly, not practiced enough.

Here's the truth: As mortal humans, we're just not good at guessing what's going on in other people's minds—well, at least not accurately. Yet it's amazing how upset we become, especially with loved ones, when they don't do exactly what we expect, even though we haven't communicated exactly what we want!

So, my counsel is this: Make it easy on yourself and others. Claim responsibility for having effective conversations by using a collaborative approach. You'll get your answer quicker, whether it's yes or no. You can then decide what you need to do to keep moving forward.

Resistance—Yours

Why do we resist asking for help?

Wanting to help others could very well be in our DNA. With rare exception, people do want to help, and they want to contribute to another's success. However, for one reason or another, we don't or can't bring ourselves to ask for this help.

Asking for help can be gut-wrenching, but what's *more* gut-wrenching is going through life with a dream or goal unfulfilled because you didn't ask for support even though you could have.

And the good news? You've got all the information and tools you need in this Step of your Success Map to ask for and get the support you need to realize more of what you want in your business and personal life. Think of all the life possibilities you have, just waiting for you to pursue!

You're now ready to ask yourself:

"Thinking of a specific action or my Intention Statement, what might cause me to resist asking for any support or resources I might need to be successful?"

_____

_____

If the cause of your resistance is not clear, review and check off which of these might be a cause for your resistance:

- "I'm not totally clear on exactly what I need."
- "I think I can do it alone."
- "I fear that person or group may say no when I ask."
- "My personal or business environment doesn't encourage asking."
- "They've said no in the past when I asked for additional resources."

- "I'm not sure I've got a good enough business case or reason for them to agree."
- "I just don't know how to ask."
- Other? _____

Find the reasons for your resistance.

James is one of those people who are gifted in many areas of expertise. He is a respected law professor for a highly acclaimed university, which he calls his "day job." He's also an exceptional lecturer on humanities and classical studies—his passion.

Even with his interesting work and other special interest hobbies, James was frustrated. My question to him was, why? His friends and colleagues all thought he had a most interesting lifestyle. James shared with me that he had grown weary of teaching law and, because of his passion for the humanities, wanted to change departments. Although this had been on his mind and in his heart for two years, he had not taken one step to make it happen. He had been feeling stuck for two years. No wonder he was frustrated.

With obvious exasperation, he confessed, "I'm running day and night juggling all of my activities, but I'm not doing what I want. If someone would give me a step-by-step plan on what to do, I'd do it. I just don't have time to figure it all out!"

In my conversation with James, it became apparent that even with all the resources he had available at his university, he had not asked anyone for assistance or support. Not one person.

James's obstacle to achieving his career change was less about his busy schedule teaching law and much more about his not asking for the support he needed from those who could give it.

Before making recommendations to James on how to stop feeling stuck and get the support he needed, we used the Problem-Solving Process to make sure he understood the underlying reasons for his resistance to asking for help.

As it turned out, James resisted asking others for the support he needed for three key reasons:

1. He was not really clear on what he wanted to do.
2. He hadn't decided where he wanted to teach.
3. He was afraid of requesting the change and receiving university or career retribution.

With that information and using the *SuccessMapping* tools, we created a Success Map to respond to those three reasons and help him to achieve his goal.

For the first reason, this was my counsel to James: "Take the first step! Decide on what you want your work life to look like, then create an Intention Statement to help you focus your thoughts and actions on achieving it."

James did this and discovered that his intention was to become a professor in Humanities at a university that would have the cultural and academic environment that he desired.

For reason number two, I suggested, "Use the Decision Matrix to decide where you want to teach."

He used the Decision Matrix in Step Seven to weigh the benefits and consequences of changing universities. James said, "Unbelievable! By using the Decision Matrix, I was able to quickly and clearly see the benefits of staying and the potential consequences if I chose to leave the university. It's amazing how long I have been in a quandary over this decision!"

James was relieved to be able to make that important career decision and with no regrets or misgivings. This allowed him to recommit to his university with a renewed enthusiasm. This took care of reason number two.

James used the Collaborative Conversation Plan to prepare for his conversation with the dean of his department. He asked for—and received—his department and university's support to change departments. He is now on track and looking forward to his *new* day job as a humanities professor. This took care of reason number three. And James achieved a life dream and his career goal.

IMPORTANT

If you find yourself resisting asking for the resources or support you need to accomplish one of your Success Map actions, question yourself about why you're resisting. Dig a little deeper. Uncover the "real cause" and then, like James, use the *SuccessMapping* tools and the actions from your own Success Map to take action and move forward.

Resistance—Theirs

Why do the people you ask for support say *no* instead of *yes*?

People resist saying yes to your requests when you have not understood or addressed the factors that help them make their decision either way, yes or no.

Whether it's one person or a group you're asking for support, people only have so much time or so many resources to support other people's business or personal goals. If you find you get resistance when you've asked someone for support, it is because:

- You have not understood or spoken to their "Yes Factors."
- You have not understood, minimized or eliminated their potential "No Factors."

Be prepared to deal with the Yes Factors and No Factors.

There are reasons why an individual or group tells you, "*Yes,* I/we will give you the additional time, money, or support you need." And there are reasons why they tell you *no,* why they are either unable or unwilling to give you what you've asked for.

The old adage "Knowledge is power" could never be truer than when you're asking others for support, time, or money.

Your odds for getting a *yes* dramatically improve when you know, plan for, and speak to your prospective helpers' Yes Factors and No Factors in your conversation. So, to improve your chances of getting a favorable response, think about what you know and don't know about the decision factors in play. Why they would say *yes*, and why they would say *no*?

Before your conversation or meeting, ask yourself, "In light of the resources or support I'm asking for, what do I know about this person's . . ."

- business environment or personal situation?

- business or personal needs, objectives, or goals that could conflict with or support mine?

- fears or concerns that might prevent this person from giving me the support I have asked for?

- decision-making process, or the influence of any third party on the decision to grant my request or not?

- other business or personal reasons that would affect why this person would—or would not—want to support me or my goal?

In business, our internal antenna is quite high—or at least it should be—when evaluating what we know and don't know about a client's business environment and even personal goals. We know it's critical to have in-depth knowledge of our clients, especially key clients, so we can protect and continue to strengthen and grow our business relationships.

We don't always have that same high antenna for other situations. So, heads up! If you are having a personal discussion with a friend or family member to ask for his or her support, or preparing for a meeting with someone inside your organization to request support with a project or a promotion, or preparing for a meeting with a financial institution or potential investor—don't abandon your high antenna for knowledge. Be prepared—know the individual's or group's Yes Factors and No Factors!

If you don't know what's *really* important to an individual or a group of decision makers when asking for their resources—STOP! Take the time and do your homework. Know what you know—and know what you don't know—about their Yes Factors and No Factors. Regardless of the effort, it pays off.

Have you ever felt (or heard someone say), "What a waste of time! I was way too prepared for that meeting?" It would be said in jest if you ever did hear it. No matter how much extra effort goes into an important conversation, presentation, or meeting, nobody is ever really overprepared.

However, what I have heard are statements like these: "I can't believe they chose his project over mine! I was totally blindsided!" "I didn't know that was how they were going to make that decision!" "If I had only known that manager was important, I would have contacted him." "Who knew she had been burned by approving this type of request in the past?" "I would have been prepared to manage that obstacle—who knew?" and a zillion more. All these statements and unfortunate outcomes could have been prevented if the person requesting support had known more about the individual's or group's Yes Factors and No Factors.

If the outcome of your conversation is not important, not to worry—don't bother, don't prepare. If it is important, however, don't wing it. Go armed with the knowledge that will help you get the support you need. Be prepared.

This personal mantra always pays off: "Prepare, prepare, prepare!"

Being prepared paid off big-time for Karen, the senior executive for the nonprofit and philanthropic services of a major corporation. Her organization walks its talk of being a good corporate citizen by contributing to several charitable organizations.

Karen discussed with me her organization's situation: "Our challenge is the same as that of any large organization—many community needs but limited resources." Then she lamented, "We get numerous requests to sponsor events, and we just can't do them all. To be as equitable as possible, an executive committee regularly meets to decide who gets the funds in each of the different categories of charities. Each corporate officer has key clients who have favored charities they believe in and support—all vying for the same limited resources. Those meetings can really get heated!"

She shared her recent experience in competing for resources. Karen had asked for—and had been granted—a significant donation to a new charity. She was told *yes*. At the same meeting, Diana—another corporate manager—was competing for the same budgeted dollars for her charity. She was told *no*.

As Karen said, "Why I got the resources was clear to everyone. It wasn't that my charity was more worthy. In fact, I volunteer my time and personally donate to the charity Diane wanted the company to sponsor. Bottom line, I was prepared for the meeting and she was not."

To help them say *yes*, have a plan for your conversation.

Karen came to the meeting with a business plan. She was well prepared to counter any reason why the committee might say no—their No Factors. She presented a business case that clearly stated the corporate and community benefits of sponsoring her charity.

Karen knew and "spoke to" the executive committee's Yes Factors. Her preparation made it easy for the committee to say yes.

When asking for resources, be prepared. Always know the answers to these two questions: "Why would they say no?" and "Why might they say yes?"

 IMPORTANT

If you have a meeting planned now to ask for resources or support from someone whose Yes Factors and No Factors you don't know, delay the meeting if you can. Don't improvise. Improvising is not a good strategy; rarely are important outcomes achieved without planning.

Even with a "gift of gab," too much is left to chance and it rarely results in effective conversations. Many business reputations have been tarnished by ill-prepared and ill-delivered presentations. So, be smart like Karen and take the time to prepare for getting a *yes*. It's worth it!

Speaking to Their Yes Factors and No Factors

On the following page are examples of Yes Factors and No Factors. When asking for resources or support from an individual or group, review the list and be prepared to both

- speak to their Yes Factors with passion and enthusiasm for what you want to accomplish; and

- minimize or eliminate any potential No Factors.

Yes Factors	No Factors
• Available resources have been identified.	• They don't have the resources you need.
• For personal or business reasons, they want you to succeed.	• They don't see the value in what you're doing.
• Ambiguity on how to help is clarified by your step-by-step plan.	• They don't know how to support you.
• They recognize your proven track record for meeting agreements and achieving goals.	• Previous experience causes them to resist.
• The potential benefit far outweighs any risk factor of time or resource investment.	• There is more risk than value for them if they say yes.
• They see a mutual benefit in the achievement of your milestone or Intention Statement.	• Your request conflicts with their other priorities.

You've covered your bases and you can confidently ask for what you need when:

- You have confirmed that "Yes, the Intention Statement I wrote in Step Two is still exactly what I want to accomplish." If not, change that statement to reflect what you now want to accomplish. Then check the actions in your Success Map to ensure that you are still on track to achieve what you want to be or do.

- You have determined what support or resources you need to accomplish each action from your Success Map.

- You have identified whom to ask and are prepared for the conversation by knowing that individual's or group's Yes Factors and No Factors.

If you don't have a plan for what you want, someone else will!

Stephen, a client who is vice president of business development for a large government contractor, expressed this concern in a recent meeting: "I'm always amazed when my staff asks for resources or career advancement without taking the time to properly prepare for the conversation. If they don't have a business case that will support a favorable decision, it's almost impossible for me to say yes to what they're asking."

He described a recent conversation with Bill, one of his program managers. Bill had requested a meeting to discuss a promotion into business development. Stephen told me, "I didn't want to disappoint him, but his lack of preparation for our meeting was evident. Unfortunately that became a key factor in my decision. It indicated to me that he wasn't ready to manage the responsibilities of the position he wanted."

Stephen continued, "Here's what I needed to hear from Bill: How much did he really know about that position's requirements? What was his plan to gain his needed experience and capabilities? What effect would his departure from his present team have on securing an important large opportunity? What were his ideas on managing that effect?" Stephen added, "And his timing for this request couldn't have been worse—right in the middle of my budget meetings. What was he thinking?"

Bill was not prepared. None of Stephen's Yes Factors and No Factors were considered or included in the conversation. Even though Stephen was not inclined to say yes to Bill's request for a promotion, he did see the conversation as an opportunity to coach Bill.

Fortunately for Bill, he had the benefit of reporting to an executive who does have an intention to teach, coach, and promote others. Because of that, Bill is now on a defined career advancement track. And Stephen freely admits, "If Bill had come in prepared with a defined plan, his readiness for what he wanted to do would have been more evident. He also would have had fewer developmental milestones to be accomplished before moving into business development."

Again (one can never hear this enough), to increase your odds of getting what you ask for, prepare for a collaborative conversation. Preparing never hurts; not preparing can.

The Collaborative Conversation Plan

Having a collaborative conversation enables you to communicate with others and accomplish something together. The Collaborative Conversation Plan (shown on the following page) is a tool for you to *plan* and *have* a conversation to enable you to ask for what you need—and get it.

When you use this conversation plan, your chances for being understood, understanding others, and getting the support or resources you need increase substantially.

When you follow the steps of the Collaborative Conversation Plan, people will recognize that you understand what is important for them and that your intention is to have a mutual-gain conversation.

A major benefit of having a collaborative approach? The other party will be more inclined to agree with you and say *yes*, a "mini-yes," to important agreements in your conversation. Examples of mini-yeses you could receive, before even asking for the needed resources or support, would be:

- Yes, what you want to accomplish—your Intention Statement—has value.
- Yes, there are areas of mutual gain (their Yes Factors).
- Yes, you have recognized and addressed any potential issues (their No Factors).
- Yes, they agree to give you the needed resources or support you requested.
- Yes, they agree to the next best action to take based on the conversation.

It's *so* much easier to gain that final *yes* agreement when the other party has given you a mini-yes to other important agreements throughout the conversation. These mini-yesses are easy to track because they follow the steps of the Collaborative Conversation Plan.

As you move through your Success Map to achieve your Intention Statement, you may have several conversations and actions to take. To help you achieve the results you want with each important conversation, review and complete the Collaborative Conversation Plan.

COLLABORATIVE CONVERSATION PLAN

Pre-Conversation:

1. Confirm what you want to accomplish, and write your Intention Statement here:

   _____

   _____

2. What specific support or resources do you need to achieve your Intention Statement?

   _____

   _____

   _____

3. Who is the best individual or group to provide that support?

   _____

   _____

4. Why might this party say *yes* or *no*? Identify the Yes Factors and No Factors:

   Yes Factors:

   _____

   _____

   No Factors:

   _____

   _____

5. What is your conversation or meeting objective? What decision or action do you want to get a *yes* decision or agreement on?

   _____

   _____

The Conversation:

1. Paint a picture for your listeners—with enthusiasm and passion—about what you want to accomplish! Share any planned actions that, when achieved, become important milestones for you to communicate and/or celebrate.

    _____

    _____

2. Why would this individual or group care or want to help? What is a mutual benefit? What would you say to speak to the party's Yes Factors?

    _____

    _____

3. How would you prove that your idea offers more value than risk? What different ideas do you have on how these people could support you? To help them help you, what would you do or say to minimize or eliminate their potential No Factors?

    _____

    _____

4. Tell them exactly what additional support or resources you need and why you've asked this person or group.

    _____

    _____

5. Be clear, concise, and specific. What exactly do you want them to do as a result of this conversation?

    _____

    _____

Post-Conversation:

1. Be sure to show appreciation for the time and effort everyone put into that conversation or meeting.

2. To keep everyone on track with agreements, do follow-up on all actions agreed to by you and them.

(See Appendix Two or go to www.successmapping.com to access an additional _Collaborative Conversation Plan_ Worksheet.)

People want to feel good about having said *yes* to helping you achieve an important life dream or goal. To reinforce and prevent any regrets over a yes decision, keep them posted on your success! Share your progress on what you set out to accomplish. With each major milestone you achieve in your Success Map, let them know how excited you are with your progress and how you continue to appreciate their support!

You are now ready to complete your Step Six Checkpoint!

step
.
six
Checkpoint

(Check the box when completed.)

You're ready to ask for—and get—what you need to succeed when you can easily answer and check each box below:

1. I do not allow any fear, self-doubt, or concern to prevent me from asking others for support or resources. If I don't get a *yes*, that *no* will be used as a stepping-stone to explore new sources of support or resources.	☐
2. I am clear and concise about what I want to accomplish. People don't have to second-guess where I am headed or how they might support my effort.	☐
3. I respect—and am mindful of—others' needs and situation, and I strive for conversations that are collaborative and have outcomes of mutual benefit.	☐

step seven

Making Decisions . . . with No Regrets!

The purpose of Step Seven in *SuccessMapping* is to help you:

- Determine which action(s) will best help you achieve your Intention Statement.

- Weigh the benefits and consequences of your chosen action(s).

- Make informed and committed decisions to move forward or not.

When you say yes, know why and mean it.
When you say no, know why and don't regret it.

WHAT TO DO? WHO TO DO IT WITH? Which direction to take? Where to start first? Should I delay this, so I can do that? Questions about making commitments to what we need to do and want to do continually arise in our business and personal lives.

There's no doubt about it: During times of rampant change and uncertainty, it's more important than ever to make the best decisions about where to invest your personal resources of time, money, and energy.

It's important to remember that, even in the bleakest economic times of business downsizing, there is still a world of possibilities and always more abundance than lack. People are being hired, new positions are being created, and new companies are being formed. People are starting new careers, using an interest or hobby as a new business venture, furthering their education, and sharpening their skills.

However, even when you know exactly what you want to accomplish—whether it is doing what needs to be done to best protect where you are now or what you're currently doing, or being promoted in your present organization, or starting your own business, or pursuing a personal life dream—certain decisions and actions may help or hinder you in achieving the results you want.

> **Success Blocker: *Decisions without foresight.*** Not weighing the benefits and consequences of important decisions and actions. Possible results? Decisions that are made with no commitment or that you later regret.

Step Seven of your Success Map will help you make informed decisions and take best actions, and know why you did so. You will be able to evaluate all the possible actions you could take to accomplish what you want and then select, commit to, and take action on what will best help.

It then becomes much easier for you to walk away, mentally and physically, from ideas, decisions, or actions that do not help you achieve your Intention Statement. Truly, this is a freeing experience. You can let go of those distracting coulda, woulda, shoulda thoughts. What a gift for your mental and emotional well-being!

Success Map Check

You've made great progress in achieving your Intention Statement! That truly is good news. So, let's check on where you are in your Success Map right now:

- ☑ You decided on a life dream or a business or personal goal that you do want to accomplish at this time. You then declared your intention to focus your thoughts and actions on achieving it, with an Intention Statement.

- ☑ You identified the obstacles that could have become stumbling blocks to keep you from moving forward and accomplishing what you want to be or do.

- ☑ You created actions in your Success Map to minimize or eliminate those obstacles, all with a mind-set of discovering new and different opportunities. And these opportunities or new resources will help you resolve those obstacles and will become stepping-stones for what you next want to achieve.

- ☑ You determined exactly what additional support you needed in order to accomplish an action to help achieve your Intention Statement. You are now prepared with a Collaborative Conversation Plan to help you ask for and get the resources or support you need from those who can help.

Wow! You've really accomplished a lot! As you've moved through the Steps of your Success Map, you've developed many new ideas and identified the decisions and actions you could take—all good. Now is the time to be selective about which of these to do, because some of your actions are more important than others for achieving your Intention Statement.

You only have one body to do both what you're doing now *and* more of what you want to do. Even if you are able to boast of mind-stretching multitasking skills, when you want to achieve something new or different it is definitely a wise strategy to make the best use of your time, energy, and brain cells!

How do you do that? Be selfish with how you employ your own personal resources. Select and commit to those actions that best help you easily and quickly achieve the results you envisioned when you declared your Intention Statement. Who's got the time or energy to waste doing the right thing but at the wrong time, or vice versa?

Completed actions are your milestones to track and celebrate your progress.

Accomplishing what you want may require two, three, or more action steps. Any action you take should help you

- move in the direction and pace you desire to achieve your goal;
- stay on track and serve as a barometer for your progress; and
- signal your accomplishments and provide a real cause for celebration.

Nancy, who was first mentioned in Step Five, overcame obstacles to going back to school and completing her education. She identified and committed to actions that, when accomplished, were major milestones by which she and her family could track her progress and success. These actions included

- completing the first semester;
- achieving a 3.5 grade average in the second semester;
- receiving a scholarship; and
- having a paper accepted for school publication.

With each accomplishment, Nancy and her family found fun and simple ways to celebrate what she was doing and her progress. Not only did Nancy get the emotional payback from her own personal satisfaction and her family's support when she achieved these important milestones, she also received a benefit that was totally unexpected.

Because her family knew about and supported her achieving her milestones, they saw how effective Nancy's Success Map had been and wanted to create their own. Nancy's modeling and success with her deliberate, step-by-step Success Map had a dynamic effect that rippled throughout her family.

For Nancy, seeing her husband and sons replicate her use of a Success Map to achieve what was important to them—with his business and their schooling—was a huge bonus.

Decisions That Keep You Moving Forward

At this Step in your Success Map, you are now ready to decide which actions to commit to and establish timelines for completing them, so that you can monitor your progress toward ultimate success in being or doing something different. These actions, when completed, are milestones that enable you to say, "I'm moving forward and right on track to achieve my Intention Statement. And I feel great about my progress!"

On completion of Step Seven, you will know the answers to the following questions:

1. Which key actions, when accomplished, become my milestones to track and celebrate?

2. Right now, thinking of what I want to accomplish with my Intention Statement, to which action should I say *yes*? And to which action should I say *no*?

David's story is a good example of how to successfully use the Decision Matrix in Step Seven of *SuccessMapping* to make tough business decisions.

David is the CEO of a high-profile and fast-growing auction house. In a recent meeting, he shared with me his business situation and some of the decisions he was considering and the actions he was taking.

In a relatively short period of time, David's company had progressed from a start-up business to one that is recognized by Fortune 100 companies as "the trusted source" to help them turn their nonperforming assets into hard cash.

How did he do this?

As most successful business people would, David had a well-thought-out business plan and strategy for how to succeed in his industry and market. Perhaps most important, he executed his plan well. Often business plans, even the best of them, can get blown up with decisions and actions that were either made too quickly or were based on emotions instead of thoughtful analysis.

David wisely said, "We have limited time and resources. We can't afford to make ill-informed or hasty decisions that could jeopardize what we want to achieve in our business and for our clients. Even in meetings when we're expected to make fast decisions, if we've not had time to really put some thought into an important decision, we'll either call a short break in the meeting or delay that particular decision. It never pays off to make ill-informed decisions."

More words of wisdom from David: "Of course, you've got to have a sound business plan. But the best plan in the world without smart execution is a guarantee for failure. Taking action on the right decision with the right people at the right time is what will differentiate you in the market and help you succeed."

Before he and his business partner started their business, they sat down and decided exactly what they wanted to accomplish. What was most important for them was not to seek additional resources but to use their own resources and knowledge in a business that was not commoditized.

Their Intention Statement: *To self-fund a business that meets our specific market criteria and growth objectives.*

Having worked with David, I can safely say that his words of wisdom had not always come easy for him. Contrary to his "make things happen" leadership style, the first major decision his company made was to do a comprehensive market and competitive analysis. Before taking any other actions, this marketplace study was the first important milestone to accomplish to achieve the business's Intention Statement.

So, as he and his partner developed their business plan, they sought answers to two critical questions:

- What business would best leverage the strengths of my financial and our technology backgrounds?

- Which industry would meet our market criteria of being behind the technology curve, not commoditized because of the glut of competition, and offering sustainable revenue growth potential?

Completing this investigation was David's first major milestone. The benefits of investing a year in market analysis were huge, as would have been the potential consequences of not having done so. The outcome of this decision set the course for the company's business and present success.

David and his partner had other actions that, when accomplished, also became critical milestones to achieving their Intention Statement:

- To have a certain number of auctions for profit and nonprofit organizations by a certain time

- To develop a specific number of key strategic and long-term client relationships

- To experience twenty-four months of projected, sustainable profits

As they continued to pursue the goals of the Intention Statement for their business, David and his partner then evaluated these key decisions:

- Do we start preparing our organization to go public now?

- Do we need to pursue outside capital to secure advanced technology and key talent?

Of the two decisions, the second—additional funding for growth— seemed the most important to decide at this time. The question that had David and his partner in a quandary was "Do we continue growing organically by self-funding, or do we change what we originally intended for our business and get additional funding from outside investors?"

Anyone who has gone down this business path knows that this is a critical decision, with the potential for huge benefits or hugely negative consequences.

Weighing the Benefits and Consequences of Important Decisions

If you tend to leap before you look, you may suffer the consequences of a rash or premature action.

On the other hand, if you tend to look, look, and look some more, and finally, as you prepare to leap, you discover there's nowhere to leap to. You could be left dismayed and wondering, "What happened? Why isn't the opportunity still there?"

Truth be told, who among us hasn't at one time or another deeply regretted leaping *or* not leaping? It can become one of those regretful couldashouldas.

Although the mental pull is strong, it's really not a good use of your time or emotions to regret any couldas or shouldas. Instead, if you catch yourself rethinking old decisions and actions, stop and ask, "What did I learn? What am I able to glean from that experience that has value for me? Was there something new or different I discovered that will help me achieve what I want to accomplish now or in the future?"

Regardless of what the outcome looks like, with a mind-set for opportunities and growth, there's always value. And that's the truth!

 IMPORTANT

When making any major decision, take time to analyze and ask, "What are my benefits and consequences of doing and not doing this action?"

The Decision Matrix: Say Yes or No, and Know Why

The Decision Matrix is the *SuccessMapping* tool that helps you quickly and confidently decide to take an action or not—and to know why. No mental twirling allowed! You either say *yes* and go for it, or say *no* and walk away, confident that you made the best decision. No regrets.

When you use the Decision Matrix, you will make decisions based on your analysis of the benefits for doing and not doing the action. This tool also identifies the consequences of doing and not doing the action.

Your decision to act or not to act becomes glaringly obvious after completing the Decision Matrix. When the *benefits of doing* and the *consequences of not doing* are stronger than the *benefits of not doing* and the *consequences of doing,* that's when you'll know to stop thinking about it, take action, and charge ahead!

If, however, the benefits of taking action do not outweigh the consequences, you may choose to either postpone that decision or choose another action with stronger benefits.

That's exactly the choice Carlos made after completing his Decision Matrix on starting his doctoral program (discussed in Step Five). During our coaching session, he quickly realized that the benefits of *not doing*—that is, not starting his degree program—far outweighed any benefit he would gain by starting the program at that time.

The Decision Matrix outcome told Carlos that it would be best to revisit this action in eighteen months. At that point, he could use the Decision Matrix to determine if the benefits for starting his doctoral program were stronger than the predictable negative consequences.

I remember him happily saying, "I can't believe it! This has constantly been on my mind. I'm always thinking, 'How can I squeeze this in with everything else going on?' Now, I can let it go with no regrets for not pursuing it at this time. I'm going to get my doctorate, just not now!"

It was interesting to watch Carlos's transformation. It appeared as though a load had been taken off his shoulders! Quite content and at peace with his decision, Carlos was now able to refocus his energy on his business and family.

The benefits you gain from using the *SuccessMapping* Decision Matrix include the following:

- Being less inclined to make impulsive or emotional decisions
- Being able to move forward or walk away from an action, knowing you've made the right decision, with no coulda-shouldas hanging on
- Being able to uncover the real reason you haven't taken action when you knew you needed or wanted to, but just never had

Here's another example: I recently decided, once and for all, that I'm going to get back into shape. "Really, this time I mean it!" This seems to be a common personal objective of many, with almost the same number of common outcomes—start, stop, procrastinate, feel guilty, eat more, ad infinitum.

Sadly, I discovered that eating less or walking faster in airports was not going to do the trick. To accomplish my intention of getting back in shape, the actions in my Success Map were:

- Get a complete physical.
- Consult with a nutritionist.
- Change my eat-on-the-run habits.
- Find a personal trainer and commit to an exercise program.

All righty! I was right on track and doing well—right up to committing to the personal trainer/exercise thing. Why all the excuses and procrastination? No time? No, although that excuse sounded good, that wasn't it. After completing my Decision Matrix, it became crystal clear why I was not regularly working out with a personal trainer.

As you can see by reviewing the sample Decision Matrix for "Exercise Program," (shown on the following page) my *benefits of not doing* and *consequences of doing* far outweighed my *benefits for doing* and the *consequences for not doing*. Well, that made me feel better; no wonder I wasn't exercising regularly.

There it was in black and white—evidence that this failure was not my fault! No wonder I wasn't committed to this part of my action plan. The consequences of exercising outweighed the benefits, so there. What a relief. No more guilt. All I really needed to do was eat less and walk faster in airports!

That rationale worked until my clothes became snugger and I was exhausted from traveling week in and week out. What was painfully obvious and most annoying was that the *consequences of not doing* exercise and the *benefits of doing* it had caught up with me. Ever experienced this?

The result: I am now the faithful companion to a personal trainer. Although reluctant for sure and not the most cheerful of her clients, I am committed nonetheless.

SAMPLE DECISION MATRIX

Action: Exercise Program

BENEFITS of Doing	CONSEQUENCES of Doing
• Get in shape	• It's boring
• Able to wear my clothes	• I could get hurt
• More energy	• Takes too much time
• Feel healthier and stronger	• Clothes and club membership are expensive

of Not Doing	of Not Doing
• Eat what I want	• Poor health
• Use the money for other things	• If I don't start now, I never will
• Sleep late	• No energy for demanding business travel
• Get to buy new clothes	• Cost and time to purchase new clothes

Confident Decisions, No Regrets!

When considering any important action, your decision should be:

- *Yes*—when the *Benefits of Doing* and the *Consequences of Not Doing* are stronger.
- *No*—when the *Benefits of Not Doing* and the *Consequences of Doing* are stronger.

Before using the Decision Matrix to help you best decide which action in your Success Map you wish to commit to, let's look at David's Decision Matrix (shown on the following page).

For more than three months he and his partner had been worrying about (and were still indecisive about) whether or not to seek outside funding to help grow their business. So, let's see how this simple analysis enabled David to quickly make a difficult decision.

SAMPLE DECISION MATRIX

Action: Secure Outside Funding for Business Growth

BENEFITS *of Doing*	CONSEQUENCES *of Doing*
• Rapid growth • Protect private assets • Business relations for future growth • New board member candidates	• Lose part or all of my business • Lose personal capital—legal fees if dispute occurs • Lose control—business direction/responsibilities • Fear of not being aligned to customer-focused culture
of Not Doing	*of Not Doing*
• Do not have to answer to anyone • In control of decisions and growth pace • More time to select right investment partner • More time available to diagnose tech needs	• Have to use personal funds • Present pace could jeopardize personal health • Not able to accomplish growth goals • Loss of diversified business acumen for board

As David and his partner discovered, having a simple process for making complex and critical business decisions can have powerful benefits.

Here are David's comments on using the *SuccessMapping* Decision Matrix:

> It's amazing—after three months of back and forth discussing pros and cons, in thirty minutes, using this decision analysis tool, we decided! We're moving ahead and will start engaging in conversations with two potential investors next week. Setting outside our fears of loss of control, the only way we can stay competitive is by continuing our growth plans and adding the technology that will support it.
>
> Our benefits for this decision and our potential consequences if we didn't go for it gave us all the evidence we needed to take action—and with no regrets for not having a business that is self-funded. It's a simple yet highly effective tool!

Moving Forward with Best Actions

As you think of accomplishing your Intention Statement, ask yourself:

1. "Which key actions, when accomplished, will become my milestones, will help me track my progress, and will be cause for celebration?"

- _____ • _____

- _____ • _____

2. "Which action do I need to assess in order to make sure that it's the best action to commit to and take, and that it will help me achieve my Intention Statement?"

   You are then ready to complete your Decision Matrix on the following page and make your decision.

   Action to assess:

   _____

DECISION MATRIX	
Action:	
BENEFITS *of Doing*	**CONSEQUENCES** *of Doing*
of Not Doing	*of Not Doing*

(See Appendix Two or go to www.successmapping.com to access an additional *Decision Matrix* Worksheet.)

3. Your decision, and why:

_____

_____

No more hesitating or regretting decisions made or not made. Using the Decision Matrix will always help you clearly see the benefits of taking an action or choosing not to do so, with no regrets.

Your time and energy can be used to celebrate each success—and then, to plan for what you next want to accomplish. No mental twirling. You're committed to the right actions at the right time, and you can now get started on achieving what you want to accomplish with your Intention Statement!

Decisions that are matters of the heart rarely need analysis. You know that life decision or action that you look back on and now say grace over because it changed your life, and all for the better. Deciding to have my son, Scott, at an early age was definitely a decision that is a gift of continual joy. No analysis needed—it was the best decision I've ever made!

Matters of the heart—committing to a relationship, having a child, caring for family members, giving time or resources to those in need—rarely need the objective analysis of the Decision Matrix. You know what feels right for you, and you just do it.

However, being the pragmatist I am, I say it never hurts to do a quick decision assessment of the benefits and consequences of any important life decision or action!

You're now ready to complete the Step Seven Checkpoint.

step seven
Checkpoint

(Check the box when completed.)

Complete each action and check the box, thinking of what you want to accomplish with your Intention Statement:

1. I have identified the key actions that are my milestones to track and, when accomplished, to celebrate. ☐

2. I used the Decision Matrix to decide which action to take now that will best help me achieve my Intention Statement. Because of this decision analysis, I'm committed to taking action on my *yes* decision, and I have no regrets for any *no* decision. ☐

step eight

Yes, I'm Really Ready to Achieve My Intention Statement!

The purpose of Step Eight in *SuccessMapping* is to help you:

- Know what to expect when leaving what's familiar and moving to what's different with each action you take.

- Recognize and take charge of the predictable change dynamics.

- Be alert to change dynamics that can sabotage being or doing what you want.

- Prepare yourself to be change-ready to move forward with actions and achieve your Intention Statement!

Critical to your success—taking charge of your thoughts, feelings, and actions that are normal and predictable with change.

WITH ANY CHANGE, WHEN YOU MOVE FROM the comfort of the old to gain the benefits of the new, the differences of the new can stop you from getting these benefits. Unless you're aware of the discomfort called *change dynamics*, it can sabotage your success.

But first, here's what you've already accomplished, and it's a lot!

You've used your Intention Statement like a personal North Star throughout your Success Map to keep you focused on your desired results. You created actions to reframe thoughts to those that will enable you to succeed, to effectively prepare for and manage obstacles, to ask for the support you need, and to act on what is important now. Step by step, you've built a solid plan that will enable you to achieve your Intention Statement.

So, what's left to do before reaping the rewards of achieving your Intention Statement?

Here's what's left: You must implement your Success Map, action by action, to get the results you want in the timeline you desire. With each action, you must not let the discomfort of any change dynamics get in the way of accomplishing your business or personal goal.

When you are asked or you choose to do something different from what is familiar, change dynamics step in. Change dynamics can be fleeting or they can absolutely consume you. Fortunately, change dynamics are easy to recognize. Whatever you are thinking and feeling will tell you exactly how you are responding to a change situation. You'll have thoughts like "What was wrong with how it was? It was working just fine. There was no need to change our relationship, or team, or responsibilities, or territory."

Of course, once you become familiar with the new, no problem. You will not continue to feel the change dynamic of grieving or hanging on to the old way, being upset or angry. Instead, you'll think, "I might not like having to do this change but it's a done deal, so how can I realize the most benefit?" You are now ready to explore the benefits of what's new because of a change.

To address change dynamics head-on, ask yourself, "With each action that I have planned in my Success Map, what might I need to do differently from what I'm doing now? How am I going to feel about that?" When you do this, you will be better prepared to manage any negative change dynamic thought or feeling. No emotional surprises or upsets for you. You will recognize the feeling for what it is—just a change dynamic to move through, not a measurement of how good or bad the decision or action was.

In theory, what you need to do differently to accomplish a life dream or goal may make total sense. Thinking about change is typically not the problem, especially if you want the change and you are excited about it. You can see yourself doing what you need to do to have that great relationship or take on those new work responsibilities. For example, seeing and thinking about what you are going to do to be a better business or personal partner is critical. But without taking action on that great vision and those thoughts, it means nothing.

If it makes sense to go through change to have the life you want, what stops you from going through change? More often than not, the change itself is not your real problem. It's not that the changes in your work or personal life are necessarily good or bad. Nope, that's not it. The real problem? The culprit? Change dynamics.

Sad but true, many of us can look back on missed life opportunities and say, "You know, he was really a neat guy. Why did I get upset and walk away so quickly?" Or, "She could have been the perfect business partner. Why did I turn down that support?" Or, "That would have been a really smart career move. I could have done that job. What was I so worried about?" We all have tons of thoughts of what we could have done but didn't do.

There also are plenty of decisions and actions we did not take and are very glad we didn't. But for those we coulda-shoulda taken but didn't, more often than not, a change dynamic is to blame.

Step Eight will fix that. This Step of your Success Map will help you have clear vision today, not just in retrospect. It will help you recognize and move through any thoughts or feelings that could prevent you from being as effective as you could be with change, and to accomplish what you want.

Don't Let the Bandits Blow Up Your Track

Imagine your Success Map looking like a train track. And on that track are all of your actions that, when accomplished, will become milestones that let you know that you're still on the right track and headed in the right direction. All the important actions in your Success Map that help you achieve your Intention Statement are train stations. At each station you do what you need to do—let people on, let people off—and keep moving forward. All is well. But uh-oh, what's this? Looks like bandits! And it looks as though they're here to blow up your track!

How you respond to a specific change can cause you to go down the track faster or can derail you or blow up your track. So, protect yourself from your own change dynamics! The key is to not allow how you respond to change to be the bandit that sabotages your success.

So, regardless of what action you're taking, whether it's starting a new relationship, accepting a new job or additional family responsibilities, seeking new resources, starting a new business venture—prepare yourself. Don't get derailed from what you want to accomplish because you need to be or do something different. If you have any resistance to doing something differently, see that resistance for what it is—just a normal change dynamic to acknowledge and move through quickly.

So, no bandits allowed. It's time to accomplish and reap the rewards of achieving your Intention Statement!

And the good news? You have full control of your change dynamics. How long you resist doing something different to achieve something new is *entirely* within your control! For example, if you fondly look back in time at how good it used to be, that's not bad—it's normal. Those appreciative thoughts for the past shouldn't keep you from changing what's needed to move forward with implementing your Success Map.

However, what *will* keep you from moving forward is getting stuck somewhere in the old when you've set your sights on something new. It's always important to remember:

- If you are grieving for how it used to be or what you thought it was, let it go.

- If you are denying having to do anything different, stop denying and start doing.
- If you are fearful to be or do things you haven't done before, do it anyway; it will get easier and you'll be wiser for it.

When you take charge of any unwelcome change dynamic that can hold you back, you'll find you have more strength and are even more determined to achieve what you set out to do with your Intention Statement.

> **Success Blocker: *Not being change-ready.*** Allowing how you respond to change to sabotage having the life you want. Not recognizing and taking charge of the predictable change dynamics.

Step Eight of *SuccessMapping* will help you go through change effectively by seizing opportunities without looking back on what you coulda, shoulda done. This Step of your Success Map will help you evaluate the following:

- Am I spending too much time grieving for the old or "how it used to be"?
- Am I hanging on to what doesn't work anymore?
- Am I denying that I need to make some changes to achieve what I want?
- Am I worrying more about what I think I can't do versus thinking about what I can do?

If your answer is *yes* to any of those questions, this is very good for you to know. That realization alone shifts your vision to take stock of what's working for you today, give thanks, and then push away from any part of your past that does not work for you anymore and take action to move forward. Do what you need to do to protect what you value today and move forward with anything you want to be different.

Regardless of the change situation, the more you know about change dynamics, the easier it is for you to get engaged quickly and be successful.

Change Dynamics—Predictable, Inescapable, Manageable

Without a doubt, with change you will experience change dynamics. It does not matter what type of change it is—huge or small, invited or unexpected, exciting or frightening, initiated by you or someone else—you will experience a *period of transition*. While it's going on, you will feel things, say things, and do things that are characteristic of change dynamics at work. How long that transition lasts and how bad it gets is up to you.

Period of transition. This is the time it takes for you to leave the old (mind, heart, and actions) and be actively engaged and successful with the new. You could have a very short period of transition or a very long one. Your change transition could last a few minutes—you've thought about it, you know what you need to do differently to succeed, and you're on it.

Or it could take months, even years to get through a difficult life-change transition period. Sometimes transitions take longer because the change may have been traumatic and our thoughts and feelings run deeper. But regardless of the cause of the transition, to experience more of what you want, the shorter the transition period, the better!

 IMPORTANT

Even when we feel change-ready, we can be quite surprised with how we actually respond when the change occurs. The moment you're asked to actually do something different is when your real transition begins and the predictable change dynamics kick in.

Predictable change dynamics. These include what we think, how we feel, and how we behave as we move from the old way of doing something to the new way. For some, going through change is not a problem. For others, needing to be or do something different from the norm can strike fear in the heart of even the bravest.

Although these behaviors and feelings are normal, if left unmanaged they can play havoc with relationships and what you want to accomplish.

As an example, let's say you've just taken a big leap of commitment with that special person in your life. You're going to get married (congratulations!). He or she is exactly who you want as a partner in your life. You've told all your friends, your family, your coworkers, and anyone else who will listen to you just how wonderful and totally perfect that person is. You're thrilled!

Heads up! Now is the time to protect your relationship from change dynamics. These are the bandits you don't want to invite on your train. Change dynamics can rob you of your joy with each other as you undertake changes in order to have the kind of relationship you want. Anytime you need to change something to benefit your relationship and you choose not to do so, consider this: You might have a bandit on your train. Resisting change, denying that you need to change, and reminiscing about pre-engagement days are all change dynamics that are threatening to blow up your track and sabotage your relationship.

Here's what can happen: Everybody is happy and all is well until you need to change something about your attitude, behavior, or actions to adapt to the new relationship. Perhaps fewer or no nights out with your old friends, more time expected to be with each others' families, more or different expectations of where you are and why you're there. Changes—some you expected and some you didn't.

You may even be thinking, "Oh my gosh, what have I done? What was wrong with the way we were? It was perfect just as it was! We were doing just fine dating. Perhaps I should postpone the wedding for a while." The doubts, questions, and fearful thoughts are now making you crazy!

It's normal!

In this scenario, even if you considered the new demands to be normal and okay, now that it's actually happening to you, they're cause for alarm. The "this is going to be different and it's making me nervous" change dynamics have kicked in. Uh-oh! Your change dynamics are attacking your train and the track you're on. At minimum it could rob you of the enjoyment of this special time in your life, and at worst it could destroy your relationship.

This does not have to be! You're okay. Your partner is okay. You're okay together.

Before you implode and destroy a meaningful relationship, put up a very high antenna for understanding what is really going on. What's happened? The normal and predictable change dynamics have kicked in. So, unless there's a reason other than change dynamics not to proceed, don't let the normal and predictable change dynamics sabotage this important time in your life.

Regardless of the type of change—going back to school, starting a new job or career, managing different responsibilities or coworkers, making a new or different commitment with a relationship, children going or coming back, moving to a new home, etc.—it's good to keep in mind: Change dynamics begin right at the moment when you leave what is familiar to start what is new or different.

Any question you may have, such as "Was this decision or action the right thing to do?" is not necessarily a bad thought to have. In fact, it might protect you from making the wrong decision. So, if you suspect this to be the case, go back to Step Seven and check it out with the Decision Matrix. Having done that, if you found your benefits for taking that action were strong, heads up! Your concern and doubt could very well be the normal change dynamics that occur when going through change.

Let It Go! Release Your Death Grip on the Old

When going through any important change, recognize any fearful or resistant thoughts and feelings for what they really are—predictable change dynamics. That way, you can manage them instead of letting them managing you.

To easily manage and quickly move through change dynamics, you must recognize, take charge of, and change any thought or behavior that does not support you in achieving your Intention Statement. So here's what to look for:

- *Emotional Crisis*—This is the first change dynamic that can hit you. Anger, anxiety, or confusion about why you are being asked to do something different is common. Time and energy can be wasted grieving for the old. Even if you didn't like the old, now that it's gone it looks pretty good! (Interesting how that happens.) It's common to miss the known old way before gaining the benefits of the new.

- *Denial*—In the second change dynamic, you're not angry or upset anymore. You've decided there's no reason to be angry or upset; besides, maybe it'll all blow over. You may think, "Maybe I won't have to do anything different. I can keep doing what I've always done and be okay."

- *Identity Crisis*—Then you realize, painfully sometimes, that denial does not work. Yes, there is change, and yes, that person or group does expect you to be engaged in making the change work. Your dominating thoughts may be "Oh no, the change is a done deal, the old is gone. I don't know if I can do what they expect of me. But I have to do something! Maybe I should leave. Is this the right, job, career, school, relationship for me?"

- *Engaged*—Now you are coming out of the mental fog of the other change dynamics! If you initiated the change, you now remember why this change was such a good idea. If you are being asked to change by a person or group, you realize that, like it or not, to be successful you need to get engaged and start seeking opportunities. There's light at the end of your change tunnel. You're engaged and accomplishing actions that need to be done to experience the possible benefits from the change.

- *The New Norm*—You've moved from the old, through the change dynamics, and into the new. Now the new is part of your norm, your new status quo. Next?

How to Recognize Your Change Dynamics

The purpose of recognizing your change dynamics? To identify any thoughts, feelings, or actions that give you the clear signal: "You are about to sabotage your plan."

Going through change dynamics is not good or bad, it just is. It's normal. But what should not be normal for you is being in a change dynamic and not leaving it. It's not good for your relationships and it will wear you out, mentally and emotionally. As you identify which change dynamic you are experiencing with a specific business or a personal change, think about what you need to do to move quickly through Emotional Crisis, through Denial, and through Identity Crisis to being Engaged as quickly as possible, so you can now claim: that change is a New Norm!

Here's the objective: To shorten how long it takes you to move from Emotional Crisis to the New Norm and not suffer by getting stuck along the way.

Before you use the How to Recognize Your Change Dynamics tool, let's look at Rich's example.

Rich is a sales representative for a computer hardware company. He and everyone in his company have been bombarded with one change after another. Now, he has another change to manage. And he's not too happy at all about it. Rich has just discovered that his boss, John, is leaving his group to manage a different sales group in his company. And one of Rich's coworkers has been named as the boss's replacement!

Rich shared with me, "Can it get any worse than this? John was so easy to work with, and now I'm supposed to report to a peer that I don't even like! That's it—I'm looking for a new job."

Let's look at Rich's analysis of how he responded to this business change. What were his change dynamics? Would his thoughts and feelings about the change—his change dynamics—help or hurt him in being successful with a change in his company that was now a done deal? His change dynamics analysis is shown on the following page.

EXAMPLE: HOW TO RECOGNIZE YOUR CHANGE DYNAMICS

Think of a current change or a change situation you expect because of an action in your Success Map. Think about what thoughts or feelings you have now or could have about that change. Then identify the change dynamic that matches your thoughts and feelings, and write them down. If you have been experiencing any change dynamic for a long time or it is continuing to deeply affect you in a negative way, you might be stuck. Preparing for how you want to respond to a new change situation will prevent you from getting stuck!

Here's how Rich worked it out:

Your Change Situation: Losing my boss and having a peer now as my sales manager!

Emotional Crisis: I can't believe John is leaving and George is taking his place. What are they thinking? George hasn't been with the company as long as I have. Why didn't they consider me? I know John and I had a few tough discussions on how I manage my time and territory, but compared to George, John was a gem. First week in his job and he's bossing everyone around, calling meetings, and demanding sales reports. He's acting like a dictator and driving everyone crazy! Everyone misses John. I certainly do.

Denial: I've got a lot of business travel coming up. I'll just keep a low profile and stay away from the office. I'll do my job and I'll avoid George as much as possible.

Identity Crisis: What am I going to do? George is asking for detailed client notes. All the important material is there, but it's in my head and notes in my customer files; I just don't have a formal process. I don't have the time to enter all this into our customer software program. Now he's talking about going on my next trip to visit my clients. John was hands-off, all he cared about was me producing the numbers. I'm not comfortable having someone monitor my client conversations. That's it—I really do need to call that sales recruiter and start looking for a new sales job.

Engaged: Maybe it's not a good time to leave the company. Besides, it's taken me four years to build my client base. Maybe I should have a conversation with George to better understand his expectations on how best to work with him. I'll also let him know about my interest in becoming involved in that new sales leadership program.

Evidence that it's now the New Norm: George was a little tough in the beginning, but now I'm used to his style of managing. He'll never be like John, but he has made some changes that have been good for the team.

You gain tremendous value when you analyze your thoughts and behaviors as you go through the normal and predictable dynamics of change. Step into your personal power—recognize the dynamics, and keep moving!

Fortunately, Rich moved past his thoughts and feelings of Emotional Crisis, Denial, and Identity Crisis and did become engaged and successful with his change situation. He took action, set up a meeting with George, and began developing a healthy business relationship with his new boss.

Rich shared with me, "Looking back on the past three weeks, it would have been much easier for me and everyone around me if I had accepted George as my new boss sooner. I spent way too long just getting over having to change!"

So, to identify how you are responding to a current change situation or to better prepare yourself for a future change because of an action in your Success Map, complete your How to Recognize Your Change Dynamics exercise on the following page. Identifying what your thoughts and behaviors could look like when you do move through a specific change helps you, when you do experience the change situation, to easily recognize that thought or feeling for what it is—not a bad change but just a predictable dynamic of the change.

EXERCISE: HOW TO RECOGNIZE YOUR CHANGE DYNAMICS

Think of a current change or a change situation you expect because of an action in your Success Map. Think about what thoughts or feelings you now have or could have about that change. Then identify the change dynamic that matches your thoughts and feelings, and write them down. If you have been experiencing any change dynamic for a long time or it is continuing to deeply affect you in a negative way, you might be stuck. Preparing for how you want to respond to a new change situation will prevent you from getting stuck!

Your Change Situation:

_____

_____

Emotional Crisis:

_____

_____

Denial:

_____

_____

Identity Crisis:

_____

_____

Engaged:

_____

_____

Evidence that it's now the New Norm:

_____

_____

(See Appendix Two or go to www.successmapping.com to access an additional *How to Recognize Your Change Dynamics* Worksheet.)

The Signs of Being Stuck

Although it's okay and normal to go through change dynamics, it's not okay for you to get stuck. Staying stuck is a showstopper. It prevents you from moving forward to be or do what you want in any aspect of your life, personally or in business.

As a consultant and coach, I've had the pleasure and the heartache of watching people in organizations all over the world rise to the occasion and excel, or fail miserably during times of change.

It's a fact: No one wants to fail! We all want to experience success in some part, if not all, of our life. So, not wanting to be successful is not the problem. Here's the problem: When asked to step up and play a different game, some choose to sit on the bench, thinking that they can play the new game with old rules by being or doing what they've always been or done. They seem to believe that they can not only survive that way but also continue to thrive.

Regrettably, some people spend an unreasonable amount of time and energy talking about and grieving for the good old days, the old boss, former colleagues, or the job that is no longer there. Strangely, when living those "good old days," we didn't think they were all that good!

I've also witnessed highly intelligent people making really unintelligent mistakes when caught in the throes of their own change dynamics. It's easy for people to fall into this trap: Some can quickly transition through the thoughts and feelings of being in the Emotional Crisis and Denial stages because of a corporate change, and then get stuck in Identity Crisis. This often happens when someone is resisting a change in leadership or has had to add or lose responsibilities.

People can begin to question their new role or potential opportunities with their present organization. And if that happens, they become vulnerable to recruitment tactics by other companies and often choose to leave for what they think will be greener corporate pastures.

Hmmm. Does it make sense to change companies because you're having Identity Crisis thoughts and feelings? Do you think any new organization you would want to work for is not going through change, too? But this is exactly what my client Bill, a regional vice president of sales for a technology company, actually did.

Bill's company was going through a massive reorganization. There was a rumor going around that the new vice president was going to merge the sales regions. So Bill decided that instead of waiting for any ax to fall on him, he would make the first move. Bill called back a recruiter who had spotted him, and he accepted a sales management position with a new company.

I spoke with Bill two months after he had moved to his new company. By then he had begun to hear about what was now happening with his now beloved and much missed old company. At his new company, he was fast becoming stuck in all the thoughts and feelings of a different change dynamic—Emotional Crisis.

Here's how Bill's conversation sounded: "What was I thinking? I didn't know that new position would become available when the dust settled from the restructure. I shouldn't have been so quick to change companies. That new regional management position would have been perfect for me and my career!"

Change dynamics strike again! Bill had allowed change dynamics to cause him to make ill-informed decisions regarding his old company, and now different change dynamics were causing him not to engage in any possible opportunities with his new company. This is a prime example of how your thoughts and feelings can manage you in a period of transition. The goal is to manage them instead.

Many of us have experienced this same scenario of moving to another company strictly because of change dynamics. Sometimes it works out well, and sometimes it doesn't. The point is that moving from one job to another while under the spell of change dynamics is rarely a good career strategy.

Even if you get caught in the drama of change dynamics and temporarily lose your bearings, it doesn't mean you won't recover. You might even go back. That's what Bill did, so there is a happy ending to Bill's story. Having learned some hard lessons, he applied for—and was hired back for—that new position. He was thrilled with the new opportunity, and his old company was glad to have him back. This scenario, of course, doesn't always have such a fortunate outcome.

So, moral of the story: When going through change, recognize and manage your thoughts and feelings for what they are—change dynamics. Manage how you react to change instead of letting any change dynamic manage you.

Being Stuck Shows!

Let's say you are stuck in Emotional Crisis. Even if you are not aware of it, it is glaringly evident to those around you—especially to those you most care about. What they see is you being upset with them (true or not) or refusing to move forward with them (true or not) to be or do something different. Unless loved ones or coworkers are clairvoyant, they may not understand that, no, you are not angry with them. You are just stuck in normal change dynamics.

Demonstrating stuck behaviors—and allowing people important to you to misunderstand the cause—for sure can play unnecessary havoc with your relationships at home and at work.

A longtime client, Carl, a business unit manager for a global equipment manufacturer, came precariously close to having his career take a wrong turn because of change dynamics. What led to his crisis situation was, simply and totally, a result of his not managing how he responded to change.

Carl, already overworked and understaffed, was asked to transfer a group of his skilled employees to another business group because of the market demands for their products. Instead of considering the business rationale of the request and making the needed business decisions, he reacted with resistance and anger and then got stuck—really stuck. And unfortunately, it was most evident to those around him. Carl engaged in emotional and angry conversations with his direct reports and with his boss and even was over-heard lamenting about the loss of key talent to an important client! Not good. Change dynamics had taken over Carl's otherwise good business reasoning.

Because of his being stuck in Emotional Crisis, especially in his highly visible leadership role, Carl's reputation was quickly being damaged. Clearly, his reaction did not represent him at his best. Fortunately for Carl, at the eleventh hour his boss stood up for him and saved him from being removed from his leadership position. Even with this show of support, Carl did have some relationship wounds to heal in his company. However, time does heal most things, and eventually the bruises from his angry confrontations with his coworkers went away.

Clearly, this was not an easy way to go through a change transition. The transition period lasted too long, and it almost had a career-altering impact.

So, here's a hard-line tip: Move through the change dynamics quickly. Get from Emotional Crisis to being Engaged as quickly as possible with no damage to you and others.

It's always good to remember that even if you are unaware of how you're managing change, others are aware of it. So take control of how you respond to change. Be and do what you need to do for yourself and with others to continue to be successful in all areas of your life.

Embrace the New and Experience the Possible

SuccessMapping Tips to Manage Your Change Dynamics

With any new personal or business change, review and apply the following tips for managing your change dynamics:

- Stay focused on your end goal. Review and use your Intention Statement you wrote in Step Two to keep your thoughts and actions moving forward.

- Move forward without delay by focusing on *why* the change has value, then on *how* you should progress and *what* you need to do next.

- Recognize when a change dynamic is causing problematic behavior, thoughts, or feelings and ask: "Is this helping me or hindering me from being or doing what I want?"

- If you want to be stuck, okay, be stuck. Just set a time limit on how long you plan on being stuck. The shorter, the better (for you!). Remember, you are in control of how you choose to respond to change!

- Immediately engage: Choose the thoughts, words, and actions that will quickly move you to finding value. If you're stuck, reflect on what you can do to quickly move through any of the thoughts or feelings of Emotional Crisis, through any Denial and Identity Crisis, to being Engaged.

- Use your *reframe* technique from Step One. Cancel any *preventing*, negative thought by reframing it to an *enabling*, positive thought.

- Abandon a focus on the past. If it doesn't serve you now, let it go. This is why it's called the "past." Generate excitement for the new possibilities—even while missing the old and before you realize the benefits of the new. This has huge value for your energy and what you next want to accomplish!

- Set milestones to celebrate your successes as you transition from the old, through the change dynamics, to the new—it's fun and it works!

Change, change, change.

Chances are you've seen your share of personal and/or business changes. Some you've managed quite well and some, well, might have been managed just a little better.

People are normally exhilarated or energized by change. However, when there's too much of it, people tend to shut down. Because of the multiple and often complex changes and all the emotional ups and downs of each impactful change, it's easy to see why people could become numb to change. That way, they avoid some of the pain, but they definitely miss all of the opportunities that change offers, too.

Even if being numb seems like a sane state of being, keep your curiosity and imagination in gear. It's always wise, regardless of whether you like the change or not, to become engaged and make the change work for you.

Know who is in control, you or your change dynamics.

You'll know the change dynamics are running you when you are mentally and emotionally *exhausted* with what seems like change on top of change.

You'll know you're taking charge of change dynamics when you're seeking personal value and feeling mentally and emotionally *exhilarated* with change. Well, okay, "exhilarated" might be a bit of a stretch, but for sure you will be satisfied with your involvement in the change!

So, instead of falling under the wheel of constant change, choose to ride. Take control of what you need to do to be successful with any action in your Success Map that may require change on your part. Recognizing how you respond to each change gives you the power to take control of those change dynamics to more easily achieve a life dream or goal!

You are now ready to complete your Success Map.

Before you set timelines to all your actions and complete your Success Map, please complete your Step Eight Checkpoint.

step eight
Checkpoint

(Check the box when completed.)

No change dynamic can sabotage your Success Map when you have answered and checked the boxes below:

1. Thinking of what I want to accomplish with my Intention Statement, I have considered which change dynamic—Emotional Crisis, Denial, or Identity Crisis—could possibly slow me down. ☐

2. Which change dynamic could slow me down, and what would I do to keep from getting stuck in that change dynamic? ☐

• Change dynamic?

• Actions?

3. What actions can I take that would be evidence to me and others that I am Engaged in making a business or personal change work? ☐

•

•

•

4. What are some ways that I can celebrate the fact that I have moved past any change dynamic that could have threatened my success? ☐

•

•

•

complete your success map
and *Make It Happen*

SO MUCH TO DO, SO LITTLE TIME! As you moved through the Steps of *SuccessMapping,* you developed a Success Map that will now be your action plan and timeline to help you next achieve what you want in the time you have.

Everything we need and want to do, today and tomorrow, is rich with challenges and opportunities. With your Success Map, you now have a step-by-step guide to help you minimize any potential business or personal challenge that could prevent you from exploring and achieving more of your life possibilities and potential.

Claiming more of your potential, what you could and should be in any aspect of your life, depends on two things:

- Believing you can
- Knowing how to make it happen

Your Success Map helps you with both. By using *SuccessMapping* as your guide and map for success, you now know, "Yes, I can. I can achieve that important life dream or goal." And with each Step Checkpoint you completed, you removed one of your eight Success Blockers.

And the best news? It doesn't stop with accomplishing this one specific goal. For all other life dreams or goals you choose to act on, you now have a solid, step-by-step map for ongoing success!

Completing Your Success Map

With your Success Map in hand, no more wishing and dreaming for what you want to be or do. You really are ready! You're prepared, and now it's time take action and make it happen. Time to move forward to accomplish what you declared you wanted in your Intention Statement.

But before you do, let's better ensure that you are totally successful in implementing and achieving your Intention Statement of your Success Map. So, consider and complete these two steps:

1. Review your decisions and actions planned in your Success Map. Use the "Success Map Review—Tips and Tools" section in this chapter for a quick review.

2. Record all important decisions and actions, and plot your timelines on your Success Map (found in Appendix Three).

Let's start with the first step.

Success Map Review—Tips and Tools

Use the following tips and tools to review the important decisions and actions you planned as you moved through each *SuccessMapping* Step and Checkpoint:

- **Tip:** Question and confirm how important and achievable what you want to accomplish in your business or personal life is, compared with other life priorities.

  Tool: For a quick goal analysis tool, use the Step One Goal Check.

- **Tip:** If you find that what you originally wanted to accomplish with your Intention Statement has changed, immediately change it and write a new Intention Statement. This keeps your energy focused on moving forward with a new Success Map and different actions.

Tool: To change your Intention Statement, rewrite what you now want to accomplish in the Step Two Checkpoint.

- **Tip:** Have a hawk eye for goal-relevant opportunities to engage in that support what you want to accomplish. With each opportunity, think of how to engage. To be engaged is to take action. To default is to let the opportunity slip by. To oppose is to purposely walk away from the opportunity.

For example: If you want that high-profile job everyone is talking about, take action on every appropriate opportunity in conversations and meetings to highlight why you're the best qualified. Deciding to wait and see what happens, whom they chose and why, only puts the outcome you wanted at risk. And to not engage with each goal-relevant opportunity can, at a minimum, lengthen how long it takes you to achieve what you want.

Tool: Thinking of what you want to accomplish with your Intention Statement, use the Your Power of Choice Exercise in Step Three to be prepared to engage in all goal-relevant opportunities.

- **Tip:** Leverage your strengths. Thinking of what you want to achieve, be aware of any "goal vulnerability" and have a survival plan. Think of how you can more easily leverage a goal-relevant personal strength to support achieving what you want to accomplish in the shortest time possible.

Tool: Use the Step Four Personal Strengths Inventory to identify your goal-relevant strengths and take action on them.

- **Tip:** Be strategic about how you manage potential obstacles. Look ahead for potential stumbling blocks, understand the causes, and prepare—in advance—the action to resolve any issues. This ensures that you stay on track with your Success Map timeline.

Tool: Use the Problem-Solving Process in Step Five to resolve or transform potential obstacles into opportunities.

- **Tip:** Do ask for needed support or resources. Hesitating, procrastinating, or just not asking can lengthen the time it takes you to accomplish what you want—or can flat-out stop you.

   Tool: Plan for and have conversations to ask and get additional resources or support. Use the tool in Step Six, the Collaborative Conversation Plan.

- **Tip:** To prevent making regrettable decisions on what action to take, weigh the benefits and consequences of taking and not taking that action.

   Tool: Use the Decision Matrix in Step Seven to quickly flush out all decision benefits and consequences before taking action.

- **Tip:** If you aren't aware of the dynamics of change, your expected Success Map timeline and plan to succeed could get derailed.

   When starting on a new or different goal, if you find your thoughts run more toward "What was I thinking? This was a terrible idea!" instead of "Even though this is different, I'm excited about the possibilities!" . . . hoist the red flag! Perhaps it was truly a bad idea, but most likely you're going through the normal mental and emotional havoc of leaving the familiarity of the old for the unknown or different of the new.

   Tool: With any important action where change is called for, use the How to Recognize Your Change Dynamics tool in Step Eight to recognize and manage any unwanted change dynamic.

- **Tip:** To more easily achieve your next business or personal goal use the *SuccessMapping* tools and Checkpoints to map your success.

   Tool: Use the Success Map in Appendix Three.
   (Go to www.SuccessMapping.com to access a free Success Map.)

Record Your Actions and Plot Your Timelines

Using the Success Map chart in Appendix Three, now record the most important decisions and actions that you need to take to achieve your Intention Statement.

Regardless of what you want to be, do, or have, there is huge benefit in being aware of and managing your Success Map timeline—the actions with each timeline that begins when you start working toward accomplishing a goal or objective and ends when you achieve it!

Decide when you're going to take the first step of your Success Map. Next, have a "best guess" date for achieving what you want to accomplish. Use the time in between to set markers for important actions and milestone achievements.

Your Success Map timeline could be as short as one or two significant conversations or quite lengthy, with several critical milestones to achieve before you reach your desired outcome.

As an example: Asking for and getting a promotion could take no more than a couple of well-planned, productive conversations with the right people. That's a short Success Map timeline.

On the other hand, if you are gainfully employed, full-time, and have visions of starting your own business or securing an advanced degree, that would require a longer Success Map timeline.

 IMPORTANT

Regardless of how long you *think* it will take to reach a desired outcome, you're in the driver's seat and in full control of how long it *really* takes. By pursuing goal-relevant activities and effectively managing important milestones you've identified in your Success Map, you can shorten your timeline!

By being aware of and managing the timeline of your Success Map, you will have:

- The ability to know "Yes, I am where I want to be," by being able to track your targeted milestones.
- The information on "How am I doing?" based on where you are in your Success Map timeline. This enables you to make the best decisions on needed actions, investment of time, or other resources.

- The knowledge to quickly discern whether or not to stop working on a current goal or to focus on a new opportunity or goal. *With a belief in having an abundance of life possibilities, be ready—there will be many to choose from!*

- The ability to clearly see how you can achieve, regardless of your life situation, more than one dream or goal—*at the same time.*

SuccessMapping the Life You Want

Now . . . just imagine the life possibilities that can happen for you if you applied the same intention and discipline of managing the actions and time-line of your Success Map to your own *life timeline*. It's a powerful thought—to think that you are going to spend your lifetime with the intention of realizing and claiming more of your life possibilities and potential!

In Step Two of *SuccessMapping*, you wrote an Intention Statement for a specific goal. Let the same intention of focusing energy and actions support you in living the life you want.

Consider this question: If you were to write Intention Statements for what is most important for you to be or do in your lifetime, what would those be?

For example, here's my life work Intention Statement: *To help others realize more of their potential.* This Intention Statement keeps me focused on making the best business and personal decisions to help me fulfill this intention.

To live the life you want, what is your business or personal life Intention Statement?

_____

_____

By knowing, writing, and declaring a life intention, you can now easily decide on the activities to pursue that best support you in living the life you intended with your life Intention Statement.

No more hesitation—just start! Use the *SuccessMapping* principles and tools to achieve what matters most to you—*it was designed for your success.*

You can achieve what you want, right now!

appendix one

At a Glance—SuccessMapping®
Step Checkpoints

**step
one**
Checkpoint

(Check the box when completed.)

1. I am aware of and have reframed my *preventing thoughts* to *enabling thoughts*. ☐

   My personal evidence of this:

   •

   •

2. I have reinforced and acknowledged those people who are supporting me in achieving what I want to accomplish. ☐

3. I have assessed the effect of those not supporting my goal at this time and will develop actions using the tools in *SuccessMapping* to help gain their needed support. ☐

4. I have completed my Goal Check analysis and will use the information to develop actions in my Success Map to achieve my desired results. ☐

   My most important goal strengths that will help me to succeed are:

   •

   •

   Actions to eliminate issues or gain support are:

   •

   •

**step
two**
Checkpoint

(Check the box when completed.)

Write your Intention Statement for what you want to accomplish: ☐

_____

_____

_____

_____

step three

Checkpoint

(Check the box when completed.)

You know you are truly aware of the impact of your choices—thoughts, behaviors, and actions—when you *answer and check each box below:*

1. In thinking of how to achieve my Intention Statement, I have considered the potential change situations and have envisioned the thoughts, behaviors, and actions that will help me move forward with what I want to accomplish. ☐

2. With each potential change situation, I have evaluated the benefits and consequences of each of my choices *to engage, to default,* or *to oppose.* ☐

3. By consciously choosing to *engage, default,* or *oppose,* I realize I am responsible for and totally in charge of my experiences and outcomes. And that is good news! ☐

4. I now understand the power and potential of my choices. And that's exciting! ☐

step four
Checkpoint

(Check the box when completed.)

By completing and checking each box, you will know you're ready to utilize or leverage the personal strengths you need to achieve any new life dream or goal.

1. I have completed the Personal Strengths Inventory and have identified my personal strengths.	☐
2. With my Intention Statement in mind, I have selected the goal-relevant strengths that best support achieving my desired results.	☐
3. With each goal-relevant strength, I have decided on which actions to take to more easily achieve my Intention Statement.	☐

step
five
Checkpoint

(Check the box when completed.)

| PROBLEM-SOLVING PROCESS | ☐ |

Write Your Intention Statement:

Obstacle(s):	Real Cause:	Possible Actions:	Best Action:

step six
Checkpoint

(Check the box when completed.)

You're ready to ask for—and get—what you need to succeed when you can easily answer and check each box below:

1. I do not allow any fear, self-doubt, or concern to prevent me from asking others for support or resources. If I don't get a *yes*, that *no* will be used as a stepping-stone to explore new sources of support or resources. ☐

2. I am clear and concise about what I want to accomplish. People don't have to second-guess where I am headed or how they might support my effort. ☐

3. I respect—and am mindful of—others' needs and situation, and I strive for conversations that are collaborative and have outcomes of mutual benefit. ☐

step
seven
Checkpoint

(Check the box when completed.)

Complete each action and check the box, thinking of what you want to accomplish with your Intention Statement:

1. I have identified the key actions that are my milestones to track and, when accomplished, to celebrate. ☐

2. I used the Decision Matrix to decide which action to take now that will best help me achieve my Intention Statement. Because of this decision analysis, I'm committed to taking action on my *yes* decision, and I have no regrets for any *no* decision. ☐

step eight
Checkpoint

(Check the box when completed.)

No change dynamic can sabotage your Success Map when you have answered and checked the boxes below:

1. Thinking of what I want to accomplish with my Intention Statement, I have considered which change dynamic—Emotional Crisis, Denial, or Identity Crisis—could possibly slow me down. ☐

2. Which change dynamic could slow me down, and what would I do to keep from getting stuck in that change dynamic? ☐

- Change dynamic?

- Actions?

3. What actions can I take that would be evidence to me and others that I am Engaged in making a business or personal change work? ☐

-
-
-

4. What are some ways that I can celebrate the fact that I have moved past any change dynamic that could have threatened my success? ☐

-
-
-

appendix
two
SuccessMapping Worksheets

GOAL CHECK

(Assess how each criterion rates, low to high, on a scale of 1–5.)

	Score each item (1–5)
What you want to accomplish: _____	
Reasons for your goal: *(Maximum score for below—10 points)* _____ _____	
Your overall ability to accomplish what you want *at this time*:	
Compatibility with other life goals:	
Priority of this goal relative to other goals:	
Availability of needed skills and competencies:	
Availability of support from others important to outcome:	
Additional time available, if needed:	
Additional resources accessible, if needed:	
Your level of commitment to this outcome:	
TOTAL SCORE: (Evaluate your score below)	
• You're ready to go. Complete a quick check on scores of 4 and below to determine if a change is needed to ensure success.	(40–50)
• Assess your 3–4 score areas to determine if a change is needed to ensure success.	(29–39)
• Question 2–3 score areas to determine significance of low score areas to your desired outcome. If important, what change is needed to ensure success?	(0–28)

YOUR POWER OF CHOICE EXERCISE

1. Your Intention Statement:

_____

_____

2. Examples of situations or opportunities to prepare for:

_____

_____

_____

3. One change situation opportunity to prepare for:

_____

_____

To _engage_:

_____

_____

_____

To _default_:

_____

_____

_____

To _oppose_:

_____

_____

_____

With each change situation, which response helps you achieve what you want to accomplish?

_____

_____

PERSONAL STRENGTHS INVENTORY

Personal Strength	Strength Description	Check if Yes
Action Oriented	decisive self-starter; less analysis; learn by trial and error	☐
Adaptable	change-receptive; flexible with ideas, people, and situations	☐
Analytical	data focused; objectively assess situations without emotion	☐
Coach	developer of others, with focus on their potential vs. lack	☐
Communicator	ability to speak, write, and explain with persuasive messages	☐
Courageous	brave; undertakes challenges; takes action without ambiguity	☐
Creative	conceptual thinking; new ideas, designs, actions	☐
Cooperative	seek mutual gain; intent on collaborative outcomes	☐
Deliberate	cautious; assess risks; due diligence prior to action	☐
Disciplined	structured; in control; timelines and metrics to mark progress	☐
Leader	vision for future; inspire others to achieve better and bigger	☐
Learner	pleasure in the process of gaining and applying new knowledge	☐
Organizer	arrange, conduct, and bring resources to plans or projects	☐
Perseverance	continue course of action in spite of difficulties; persistent	☐
Positive	enthusiastic; outlook of good (vs. bad) in people and situations	☐
Problem Solver	the fixer; energized by analyzing and finding solutions	☐
Relationship Oriented	social; caring of others; energized by old and new relationships	☐
Resourceful	ability to use resources wisely; avoid waste of assets	☐
Responsible	take ownership; choose to be accountable for actions	☐
Result Driven	quest for achievement and energized by accomplishments	☐
Self-Assured	confidence in own decisions, ability, and talents	☐
Strategic	analyze relevant elements, then create an actionable plan	☐
Take-Charge Oriented	assertive, risk tolerant, independent; less need for consensus	☐
Tolerant	open-minded, patient, unbiased toward others	☐
Values-Based	conscientious; values/beliefs of family, spirituality, high ethics	☐

USING YOUR PERSONAL STRENGTHS
TO ACHIEVE YOUR INTENTION STATEMENT

Write Your *Intention Statement* Here: (Step Two Checkpoint)

Goal-relevant strength	What thought or action would utilize or leverage this strength?

PROBLEM-SOLVING PROCESS

Write Your Intention Statement:

Obstacle(s):	Real Cause:	Possible Actions:	Best Action:

COLLABORATIVE CONVERSATION PLAN

Pre-Conversation:

1. Confirm what you want to accomplish, and write your Intention Statement here:

   _____

   _____

2. What specific support or resources do you need to achieve your Intention Statement?

   _____

   _____

   _____

3. Who is the best individual or group to provide that support?

   _____

   _____

4. Why might this party say *yes* or *no*? Identify the Yes Factors and No Factors:

   Yes Factors:

   _____

   _____

   No Factors:

   _____

   _____

5. What is your conversation or meeting objective? What decision or action do you want to get a *yes* decision or agreement on?

   _____

   _____

The Conversation:

1. Paint a picture for your listeners—with enthusiasm and passion—about what you want to accomplish! Share any planned actions that, when achieved, become important milestones for you to communicate and/or celebrate.

_____

_____

2. Why would this individual or group care or want to help? What is a mutual benefit? What would you say to speak to the party's Yes Factors?

_____

_____

3. How would you prove that your idea offers more value than risk? What different ideas do you have on how these people could support you? To help them help you, what would you do or say to minimize or eliminate their potential No Factors?

_____

_____

4. Tell them exactly what additional support or resources you need and why you've asked this person or group.

_____

_____

5. Be clear, concise, and specific. What exactly do you want them to do as a result of this conversation?

_____

_____

Post-Conversation:

1. Be sure to show appreciation for the time and effort everyone put into that conversation or meeting.

2. To keep everyone on track with agreements, do follow-up on all actions agreed to by you and them.

DECISION MATRIX

Action:

BENEFITS *of Doing*	CONSEQUENCES *of Doing*

of Not Doing	*of Not Doing*

EXERCISE: HOW TO RECOGNIZE YOUR CHANGE DYNAMICS

Think of a current change or a change situation you expect because of an action in your Success Map. Think about what thoughts or feelings you now have or could have about that change. Then identify the change dynamic that matches your thoughts and feelings, and write them down. If you have been experiencing any change dynamic for a long time or it is continuing to deeply affect you in a negative way, you might be stuck. Preparing for how you want to respond to a new change situation will prevent you from getting stuck!

Your Change Situation:

_____

_____

Emotional Crisis:

_____

_____

Denial:

_____

_____

Identity Crisis:

_____

_____

Engaged:

_____

_____

Evidence that it's now the New Norm:

_____

_____

appendix three

success map

success
map

Intention Statement of what you want to accomplish: _____

_____

SUCCESS MAP TIMELINE   **Start:**   **Finish:**

SuccessMapping Step or Checkpoint	Action	Support or Resources Needed

Who is the Best Person or Group to Ask	Success Map Action Timelines	
	When to Start the Action	When the Action is Completed
		☐
		☐
		☐
		☐
		☐
		☐
		☐
		☐
		☐
		☐
		☐
		☐

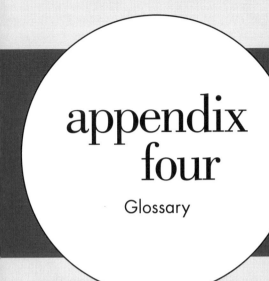

appendix four

Glossary

Benefits and consequences: Used in the Decision Matrix to assess the value of doing and/or not doing a specific action.

Bona fide strength: A personal strength that is preferred and used frequently.

Checkpoints: Stops at the end of each *SuccessMapping* Step, to track and monitor your progress before moving to the next Step.

Collaborative Conversation Plan: A mutual-gain conversation plan to more easily and effectively ask for and get any resources or support needed to accomplish your goal.

Collective challenge: Group or organizational issue or problem.

Crawdaddin': *Backing up* from a previous statement or belief.

Decision Matrix: A decision-making tool—best decisions, yes or no, made with no regrets.

Default: A response-to-change choice—choosing to do nothing, to wait and see or protect the status quo.

Denial: A predictable change dynamic—thinking there is no need to do anything different to protect what you have or achieve something different.

Emotional Crisis: A predictable change dynamic—stalled on taking any action because of fear, anxiety, or confusion over questions of why, how, or what to do first. Or missing the known elements of the old before gaining the benefits of the new.

Enabling thoughts: Positive thoughts that support you in achieving what you want.

Engaged: A predictable change dynamic and response-to-change choice—to move forward, be involved, take action.

Goal Check: A tool used to assess the importance and achievability of any goal or objective.

Goal-death alert: The thoughts or words that let you and others know you are not pursuing an important business or personal goal.

Goal-relevant strength: Your personal strengths that are most relevant to helping you achieve a specific goal.

Identity Crisis: A predictable change dynamic—with realization that the old is gone, you're over being angry and upset and denial didn't work. You're now questioning whether the new situation is right for you.

Intention Statement: A declaration that focuses thoughts, behavior, and actions on achieving specifically what you next want to accomplish.

New Norm: A predictable change dynamic—after moving through a change transition, now being engaged in the new.

Oppose: A response-to-change choice—to resist in thought or action, moving in the opposite direction.

Personal power: Choosing to celebrate what works and change what doesn't; being conscious and responsible for thoughts, speech, and actions.

Personal strength: Something you enjoy doing, you look forward to doing again and again, and you miss doing if you're not doing it enough.

Pipe dream: A goal or objective that is more than a "stretch" and is hard to imagine actually achieving.

Potential: The human and extraordinary realm of life possibilities.

Predictable change dynamics: The normal and predictable thoughts, behaviors, and actions that occur when going through change.

Preventing thoughts: Negative thoughts that prevent you from achieving what you want.

Problem-Solving Process: A four-step process to identify and understand the real cause of any potential goal or objective obstacle.

Reframe: Consciously choosing to change a negative thought to a positive thought.

Response-to-change choices: With each change opportunity, choosing to engage, to default, or to oppose being involved.

Restructure: To reorganize or streamline.

Scope: Range or capacity.

Stepping-stone: An obstacle or stumbling block that is transformed to a new way of thinking or the discovery of new or different support, relationships, or paths to needed resources.

Stepping up: Choosing to engage or take action.

Stumbling blocks: Potential obstacles to achieving what you want.

Success Blockers: The eight major reasons that stop you from starting and completing something you set out to achieve.

Success Map: A step-by-step, start-to-finish, how-to map for individual achievement. A map of best decisions and actions developed by moving through each Step and Checkpoint of *SuccessMapping,* with timelines to achieve a specific business or personal goal.

***SuccessMapping* Steps:** The eight chapter Steps that remove the eight Success Blockers and help you complete your Success Map to achieve what you want to accomplish.

Transition period: The time it takes between leaving the familiar of the old and being engaged in the new.

Yes/No Factors: When requesting needed support or resources—these are the reasons why an individual or group tells you *yes* or *no.*

Acknowledgments

My heartfelt gratitude to:

All of my clients, colleagues, friends and family who shared their experiences, dreams and goals and breathed life into each step of *SuccessMapping*.

Jim Sturdivant, your creative mind and zest for research helped set concept direction.

Alice Adams, a gifted editor with a vision for life's possibilities. You set the milestone markers and kept me in production mode from the beginning. Your friendship and contribution were truly invaluable.

All of the extraordinarily talented and committed team at the Greenleaf Book Group. Special thanks to Bill Crawford, you are an extraordinary person and brilliant editor. You added immeasurable value to the core concepts of *SuccessMapping*. And, you are a delight to work with! Tanya Hall, a successful combination of savvy business woman and personal consultant. Chris McRay, my project manager, demonstrated great patience and expertise as he handled the book production process. And Sheila Parr, designer extraordinaire who designed what I consider to be an award winning book cover and interior design. To all, your flexibility and drive for the best was always evident, thank you.

My master-mind group of highly successful and life motivated people, Diane Eichenbaum, Grady Smart, Linda Wind and Nancy Marlowe. All concerns and fears were lifted with your powerful love, support and friendship.

My parents Thomas Bell and Joyce Hunt, your love and life teachings enabled me to strive to realize more of my potential. Tommy and Kelley Bell, you are both role models in all you do, as a couple, as parents and as a supportive brother and sister-in-law. Your thoughtful input into the book was so very important.

My son, Scott Johnson, you are a continual blessing and source of pride in who you are and all you do. Your loving support, patience and wise counsel were always target-on. With much thanks to my daughter-in-law, Sue Johnson, a gifted teacher and loving mother. Braden Johnson, Sarah Johnson and Blake Johnson, you are what matters most. I love and appreciate you all.

About the Author

ARLENE JOHNSON, FOUNDER AND PRESIDENT of Sinequanon Group, Inc., is an internationally known speaker, author and consultant with more than two decades of experience in executive leadership, change management, and performance coaching. Through her efforts, major corporations as well as small and mid-sized companies create a results-oriented and competitive difference in demanding, radically changing business environments.

As president of SGI, Dallas, TX, Arlene has used her extensive business background and affiliate partnerships to help organizations optimize sales and change leadership performance. As a performance consultant, she has worked with a broad range of companies in the oil and gas, aerospace, utilities, telecommunications, financial, and health industries. Her wide-ranging expertise and unique approach have led client companies as well as executive leadership in accomplishing extraordinary results.

She has advised Fortune 500 clients such as Arco Pipeline (Corporate and Jakarta, Indonesia), American Express (Mexico), Hewlett-Packard, (Hong Kong), Hill-Rom, Southern Methodist University, Bombardier Aerospace, Texas Instruments, Fidelity Investment, Equifax (Canada), Blue Cross and Blue Shield, BDO Seidman, John Zink Company, LLC, Alcatel-Lucent, Lockheed Martin, and numerous other fast-growing, entrepreneurial companies.

Arlene has served on the executive committees of the Dallas Chapter of the United Nations Association and the Sales and Marketing Executives Association and as member of the Conflict Resolution Network of Australia. She is also involved in various nonprofit organizations.

Her special interests include travel, the fine arts, reading, and time spent with family.

To further expand how you can experience more of your life's possibilities.

www.SuccessMapping.com

****

Online you will be able to:

- Free Download
  - ○ Success Map
  - ○ Eight SuccessMapping Checkpoints
- Attain *SuccessMapping* Worksheets
- Listen to excerpts from *SuccessMapping* audio clips.
- Order additional copies of *SuccessMapping* for customers, colleagues and family members.
- Review articles and podcasts on individual and organizational success how-to's and performance.
- Learn how to book Arlene for a speaking engagement.
- Learn how to bring the following training to your group or organization
  - ○ *SuccessMapping—Success Map Workshops*
  - ○ *Consultative Customer Conversations*
  - ○ *Strategic Selling*
  - ○ *Principled Negotiations*
- Access success tips, best practices and new resources
- Continue to realize more of your potential!

Arlene Johnson • Sinequanon Group Inc • www. SinequanonGroup.com
www.SuccessMapping.com - 888-991-6992 • info@sgroupinc.com